GRANDMOTHER'S BEST COOKBOOK

GRANDMOTHER'S BEST COOKBOOK

Homemade and much-loved recipes from Grandmother's Kitchen

First published in 2011
LOVE FOOD is an imprint of Parragon Books Ltd

Parragon
Queen Street House
4 Queen Street
Bath BA1 1HE, UK

ISBN: 978-1-4454-3805-4

Printed in China

Introduction and Grandmother's tips written by Linda Doeser
New recipes written by Beverly LeBlanc
Edited by Fiona Biggs
Additional photography and styling by Mike Cooper
Additional home economy by Lincoln Jefferson
Designed by Sarah Knight

Notes for the Reader
This book uses both metric and imperial measurements. Follow the same units of measurement
throughout; do not mix metric and imperial. All spoon measurements are level: teaspoons are assumed to
be 5 ml, and tablespoons are assumed to be 15 ml. Unless otherwise stated, milk is assumed to be whole,
eggs are large, individual vegetables are medium, and pepper is freshly ground black pepper.
The times given are an approximate guide only. Preparation times differ according to the techniques used
by different people and the cooking times may also vary from those given. Optional ingredients, variations,
or serving suggestions have not been included in the calculations.
Recipes using raw or very lightly cooked eggs should be avoided by infants, the elderly, pregnant women,
convalescents, and anyone with a chronic condition. Pregnant and breastfeeding women are advised
to avoid eating peanuts and peanut products. People with nut allergies should be aware that some of
the prepared ingredients used in the recipes in this book may contain nuts. Always check the packaging
before use.
Vegetarians should be aware that some of the ready-prepared ingredients used in the recipes in this book
may contain animal products. Always check the packaging before use.

Picture acknowledgments
The publisher would like to thank the following for permission to reproduce copyright material:
Page 5: stack of cups and saucers © Alexandra Grablewski/Getty images
Vintage labels © AKaiser/Shutterstock
Close-up notepaper on cork board © Picsfive/Shutterstock
A coffee cup stain © Tyler Olson/Shutterstock
Masking tape © Samantha Grandy/Shutterstock
Vintage prints supplied courtesy of Istock Images

Contents

INTRODUCTION

When we are young children we love our grandmothers unquestioningly, delighting in their undivided attention, their patient willingness to show us how to make cupcakes, the songs and rhymes they know, and the stories of when they were little girls. Sadly, as we grow into adulthood and we become increasingly busy and preoccupied with our careers and children of our own, we can sometimes become a little bit dismissive of the older generation. But grandmothers have a wealth of knowledge and experience to draw on—from preparing a celebration dinner so that everything is ready at the same time, to tempting the appetite of a sick child with homemade soup, and from stocking the pantry with a fabulous array of jellies and preserves, to providing nutritious and tasty family meals all year round.

In fact, the grandmother in the family is its greatest resource. Not only has she acquired knowledge and experience in numerous aspects of life, from raising a family to fixing a faulty faucet, she is also the repository of family wisdom, having learned much from her own grandmother and mother. Moreover, people live longer these days, so many families are blessed not just with an active and vigorous grandmother, but a lively great-grandmother too. Of course, not everything these matriarchs have learned over the years is appropriate to twenty-first-century life. Cleaning rugs by sprinkling them with damp tea leaves, then sweeping with a stiff broom is hardly fitting in the twenty-first century when tea comes in bags and

everyone has a vacuum cleaner. However, much remains pertinent, whether it's how to manage a balanced family diet or a balanced family budget.

Today's grandmothers are not little gray-haired old ladies, knitting in a fireside rocking chair. In their younger days, modern grandmothers have witnessed great changes in the world and have been quick to take advantage of the best, most useful, and most practical of them—whether buying noniron fabrics, going late-night shopping, making good use of the freezer, or speeding up cooking in a microwave oven. Many of them had jobs outside the home and found ways to balance work and family life, and most have had to cope with a few rough patches along the way.

Make the most of your matriarch

No one ever really learns from someone else's mistakes, but everyone can benefit from the things someone else got right. Not every grandmother was a rocket scientist, but practically all grandmothers have acquired a vast amount of information and experience that has direct relevance to family life. When your little angel who always shared her toys and slept through the night suddenly turns into a tantrum thrower who won't eat her greens, trust your grandmother when she says that nothing in childhood lasts and this too will change.

These days there are hundreds of thousands of books and probably millions of Web sites to turn to when you need the answer to a problem that is bothering you or you simply don't know how to do something. But how do you know that they are right? When your grandmother comes up with an answer, you know that she's been there and done that. Why does she make the best gravy in the world? Probably because she got it wrong a few times, but too long ago to bother about now.

(Scrape up the sediment off the bottom of the roasting pan with a wooden spoon as the liquid cooks, add a splash of wine to give it the richest flavor, and keep stirring.) Why is her pastry so crisp and melt-in-the-mouth? (She rinses her hands under cold water and handles the dough as little as possible so that the fat—butter, always butter—doesn't melt.) Why are her sweaters so soft? (She reads and follows the washing instructions, even when it says hand wash!)

Most grandmothers don't realize just how much they know. They know practical things, such as how to blend together a quick, tasty, and nourishing snack in the blender with some fresh or frozen berries, a spoonful of honey, and a container of plain yogurt; useful facts, such as the ideal, safe temperature for a refrigerator is 40°F/4°C; clever tricks, such as adding two or three clean tennis balls to the dryer when drying pillows or comforters to prevent the filling from becoming lumpy; and time-saving tips, such as using kitchen scissors to chop herbs, anchovy fillets, ham, bacon, scallions, sundried tomatoes, and pitted olives.

From Grandmother with love

Probably the very best thing about grandmothers is that they will do things for their children and their grandchildren that they would never have the time, patience, or inclination to do for anyone else in the world. Mom is often stressed and pressed for time, racing home after work, picking up the kids on the way, assembling the family meal before bedtime, and then folding and ironing the laundry. But grandmothers know that a preschooler can spend a totally fascinated—and astonishingly quiet—half hour shucking fresh peas and, of course, will happily eat the fruits of his or her labor at dinner. Grandmothers will always find time to do it—as well as making sandwiches stamped into moons and stars with cookie cutters.

Grandmothers love to share a weekend lunch or, better still, a celebration meal with the family and show off the culinary skills acquired during a lifetime of cooking—whether the menu is simple fare or classic family dinners. And any family in its right mind will relish these occasions too. The meal may not match the flamboyant and extravagant dishes of television's master chefs, but will invariably have been prepared with loving care and with a special eye on who likes what—only a grandmother can do that. Grandmothers know that people always appreciate food made with love, so take a leaf out of your grandmother's book—whenever you're baking or making jellies or preserves, make an extra batch or fill an extra jar, then package it up with style by cutting out and sticking on  one of the labels on pages 217–221. The labels can also be used as gift tags to add a personal and pretty touch, turning your homemade creations into a gift anyone would be happy to receive.

Grandmothers passionately—maybe overenthusiastically sometimes—want to pass on all the things they have learned in their long lives, whether firsthand or at their own grandmother's knee: a pinch of cayenne pepper adds a delicious kick to a cheese sauce, halving vegetables and then slicing them flat side down prevents the knife from slipping, cleaning the refrigerator with a solution of baking soda avoids residual soapy smells, and it's okay to play some music and dance in the yard with the children late on a sunny Friday evening because they don't have to get up for school in the morning.

Grandmothers, it's true, don't know everything, although they know a lot. Every grandmother hopes that her daughters and daughters-in-law will value her wisdom and the wisdom of all the grandmothers who have gone before and add to it as they reach that marvelous stage of life when they become grandmothers themselves.

TRIED & TRUE
FAVORITES

Chicken Noodle Soup

SERVES 4–6
INGREDIENTS

- 2 skinless chicken breasts
- 5 cups water or
  chicken stock
- 3 carrots, peeled and cut
  into ½-inch/1-cm slices
- 3 oz/85 g vermicelli
  (or other small noodles)
- salt and pepper
- fresh tarragon leaves,
  to garnish

1 Place the chicken breasts in a large saucepan, add the water, and bring to a simmer. Cook for 25–30 minutes. Skim any foam from the surface, if necessary. Remove the chicken from the pan and keep warm.

2 Continue to simmer the liquid, add the carrots and vermicelli, and cook for 4–5 minutes.

3 Thinly slice or shred the chicken breasts and place in warmed serving dishes.

4 Season the soup with salt and pepper to taste and pour over the chicken. Ladle into warmed bowls and serve garnished with the tarragon.

GRANDMOTHER'S TIP
Clean hands are the best tools for shredding cooked chicken, flaking cooked fish, crumbling cheese, and tearing delicate salad greens and herbs.

Potato Pancakes

MAKES 12 PANCAKES

INGREDIENTS

- 4 large potatoes, peeled and coarsely grated
- 1 large onion, grated
- 2 extra-large eggs, lightly beaten
- ⅓ cup fine matzo meal
- 1 tsp salt
- pepper
- sunflower oil, for frying

TO SERVE
- sour cream
- thinly sliced smoked salmon
- snipped chives

1 Preheat the oven to low and line a heatproof plate with paper towels. Working in small batches, put the potatoes on a dish towel, then gather up the edges of the dish towel and squeeze to extract as much water as possible. Put the potatoes in a large bowl, add the onion, eggs, matzo meal, salt, and pepper to taste, and mix together.

2 Heat a large, heavy-bottom skillet over medium–high heat. Add a thin layer of oil and heat until hot. Drop 2 tablespoons of the mixture into the skillet and flatten slightly. Add as many more pancakes as will

fit without overcrowding the skillet. Fry for 2 minutes, or until crisp and golden underneath. Flip or turn, using a spatula, and continue frying for an additional 1–2 minutes, until crisp and golden.

3 Repeat this process using the remaining batter. Meanwhile, transfer the cooked pancakes to the prepared plate and keep warm in the preheated oven. Add extra oil to the skillet between batches, if necessary. Serve the pancakes hot, topped with sour cream and smoked salmon, and sprinkled with snipped chives.

IDEAL LIGHT BITE

Old-Fashioned Chicken Stew

SERVES 6

INGREDIENTS

- 2 tbsp vegetable oil
- 1 whole chicken, weighing 4–5 lb/1.8–2.25 kg, cut into quarters, backbone reserved
- 4 cups chicken broth
- 3 cups water
- 4 garlic cloves, peeled
- 1 bay leaf
- 4 sprigs fresh thyme
- 5 tbsp butter
- 2 carrots, cut into ½-inch/1-cm pieces
- 2 celery stalks, cut into ½-inch/1-cm pieces
- 1 large onion, chopped
- 5 tbsp flour
- 1½ tsp salt
- dash of hot sauce
- pepper

DUMPLINGS

- 1¾ cups all-purpose flour
- 1 tsp salt
- 2 tsp baking powder
- ¼ tsp baking soda
- 3 tbsp cold butter
- 2 tbsp thinly sliced scallion tops
- 4 tbsp buttermilk
- ¾ cup milk

1 Put the oil in a Dutch oven over high heat. Add the chicken pieces and brown, then add the broth, water, garlic, bay leaf, and thyme. Bring to a boil, then reduce the heat to medium and simmer, covered, for 30 minutes. Uncover, transfer the chicken to a bowl, and let cool. Strain the cooking liquid into a separate bowl, skimming off any fat that rises to the top.

2 Add the butter, carrots, celery, and onion to the Dutch oven and sauté for 5 minutes before carefully stirring in the flour. Cook for an additional 2 minutes, then whisk in the reserved cooking liquid, 1 cup at a time. Add the salt, hot sauce, and pepper to taste. Reduce the heat to low and simmer, covered, for 30 minutes, until the vegetables are tender.

3 Remove the chicken meat from the bones and tear into chunks. Stir the chicken pieces into the cooked vegetables. Cover and reduce the heat to low.

4 To make the dumplings, put the flour, salt, baking powder, and baking soda into a mixing bowl and stir. Add the butter and cut in until the mixture resembles coarse breadcrumbs. Add the scallion tops, buttermilk, and milk and stir with a fork until a thick dough forms.

5 Stir the stew and drop large balls of the dumpling dough into the mixture. Cover and cook for 15 minutes over medium heat. The dumplings are done when they are firm and cooked in the center. Turn off the heat and serve in warmed bowls.

Biscuits & Gravy

MAKES 12

INGREDIENTS

- 3 cups all-purpose flour, plus extra for dusting
- 1 tbsp baking powder
- 1½ tsp sugar
- ¾ tsp salt
- ½ tsp baking soda
- ¾ cup butter, chilled and diced, plus extra to serve
- 1¼ cups buttermilk, plus extra if needed

GRAVY

- 1 lb/450 g Italian bulk sausage
- 2 tbsp beef drippings, pork drippings, lard, or sunflower oil
- 3 tbsp all-purpose flour
- 1½–2 cups milk
- cayenne pepper, to taste (optional)
- salt and pepper

1 Preheat the oven to 425°F/220°C and lightly dust a cookie sheet with flour. Put the flour, baking powder, sugar, salt, and baking soda into the bowl of a food processor and blend until blended. Add the butter and lightly blend until the mixture resembles coarse breadcrumbs. Turn out into a large bowl and make a well in the center. Pour 1 cup of the buttermilk into the well and, using a fork, lightly blend until the mixture comes together, adding extra buttermilk, a tablespoon at a time, if necessary.

2 Turn out the mixture onto a floured counter and pat into a rough dough. Dust a rolling pin with flour and roll out the dough to a thickness of 1 inch/2.5 cm. Using a floured 2½-inch/6-cm round cookie cutter, cut out 12 biscuits, pressing straight

down with the cutter. Reroll the trimmings, if necessary, handling the dough as little as possible. Arrange the biscuits on the cookie sheet, pressed next to each other, prick the tops, and brush with any remaining buttermilk. Bake in the preheated oven for 15–18 minutes, until well risen and golden brown.

3 Meanwhile, to make the gravy, put the sausage in a skillet and cook over medium–high heat, breaking up the meat with a wooden spoon, until browned and cooked through. Using a slotted spoon, remove the meat and set aside.

4 Add the drippings to the skillet and heat. Sprinkle over the flour and stir for 2 minutes. Add the milk, stirring, until the gravy is thick and smooth. Return the meat to the skillet and heat through. Season with salt and pepper to taste, adding cayenne pepper, if using.

5 Split the hot biscuits, then butter them and serve immediately, with the gravy spooned over.

GRANDMOTHER'S TIP
Add the buttermilk slowly, mixing in each addition well before adding more. If the dough is too wet, it will be impossible to roll out.

Parker House Rolls

MAKES 12 ROLLS
INGREDIENTS

- ½ cup milk
- 4 tbsp water
- 5 tbsp butter, softened, plus extra for brushing
- 2½ cups white bread flour, plus extra for dusting
- 2¼ tsp active dry yeast
- 1 tbsp sugar
- ½ tsp salt
- 1 extra-large egg, beaten
- sunflower oil, for greasing

1 Put the milk, water, and 2 tablespoons of the butter into a small saucepan and heat to 110–120°F/43–45°C. Put the flour, yeast, sugar, and salt into a large bowl, stir, and make a well in the center. Slowly pour in 6 tablespoons of the milk mixture, then add the egg and beat, drawing in the flour from the side. Add the remaining milk, tablespoon by tablespoon, until a soft dough forms.

2 Grease a bowl and set aside. Turn out the dough onto a lightly floured counter and knead for 8–10 minutes, until smooth and elastic. Shape the dough into a ball, roll it around in the greased bowl, cover with plastic wrap, and set aside for 1 hour, or until doubled in size.

3 Turn out the dough onto a lightly floured counter and punch down. Cover with the upturned bowl and let rest for 10 minutes. Meanwhile, preheat the oven to 400°F/200°C and dust a cookie sheet with flour. Melt the remaining butter in a small saucepan over medium heat.

4 Lightly flour a rolling pin and use to roll out the dough to a thickness of ¼ inch/5 mm. Using a floured 3¼-inch/8-cm round cookie cutter, cut out 12 circles, rerolling the trimmings, if necessary. Brush the middle of a dough circle with butter. Use a floured chopstick or pencil to make an indentation just off center, then fold along that indentation and pinch the edges together to seal. Place on the prepared cookie sheet, cover with a dish towel, and let rise while you shape the remaining rolls.

5 Lightly brush the tops of the rolls with butter and bake in the preheated oven for 12–15 minutes, until the rolls are golden brown and the bottoms sound hollow when tapped. Transfer to a wire rack to cool. Serve warm or at room temperature.

GRANDMOTHER'S TIP
You can make these rolls in large batches, then freeze for up to 6 months. They will defrost quickly at room temperature and should be eaten as soon as possible to avoid drying out.

Turkey & Dressing

SERVES 8–10
INGREDIENTS

- 10-lb/4.5-kg oven-ready turkey, rinsed and patted dry
- 2 garlic cloves, sliced
- 1 orange, sliced
- 4 tbsp butter, melted, for brushing
- salt and pepper

SAUSAGE & FRUIT DRESSING

- 1 lb/450 g spicy Italian bulk sausage
- 4 tbsp butter, plus extra for greasing
- 3 celery stalks, finely chopped
- 1 onion, finely chopped
- 6 slices day-old bread, crusts removed and cubed
- ½ cup turkey stock or vegetable stock, plus extra if needed
- 1 cup dried fruit, such as currants, raisins, and golden raisins
- 1¼ cups coarsely chopped fresh cranberries
- ¼ cup finely chopped fresh parsley
- 2 tsp dried thyme
- 1 tsp dried sage
- finely grated zest and juice of 2 large oranges
- salt and pepper

1 To make the sausage and fruit dressing, put the sausage into a skillet over medium–high heat and fry, breaking it up with a wooden spoon, until browned. Remove the meat and pour off the fat. Melt the butter in the skillet, add the celery and onion, and fry, stirring, for 3–5 minutes, until softened. Add the bread and stir until it starts to brown, then add the contents of the skillet to the sausage. Stir in the stock, dried fruit, cranberries, herbs, and orange zest. Add enough orange juice to make a moist stuffing and season with salt and pepper to taste. Use immediately or let cool completely and chill in the refrigerator until required. Bring to room temperature before using.

2 Preheat the oven to 350°F/180°C and grease a baking dish. Fry a little dressing to taste for seasoning and adjust, if necessary. Use to stuff the neck end of the turkey, securing the skin over the opening with wooden toothpicks. Put the garlic and orange slices into the cavity and truss the legs together.

3 Weigh the stuffed bird and calculate the cooking time at 20 minutes per 1 pound/450 g plus 20 minutes. Place the bird, breast side up, on a roasting rack in a roasting pan, smear with butter, and sprinkle with salt and pepper. Cover loosely with foil and roast for the calculated time, or until the juices run clear when you pierce the thighs with a skewer.

4 Remove the turkey from the oven and let rest, covered, for 30–45 minutes before carving. Meanwhile, cover the dish of dressing with foil and roast in the oven for 20–25 minutes. Carve the turkey and serve, accompanied by the dressing.

GRANDMOTHER'S TIP
To give the turkey time to come to room temperature, remove it from the refrigerator 1 hour before you're ready to start cooking.

Chicken-Fried Steak

SERVES 4

INGREDIENTS

- 4 beef cube steaks, 6 oz/175 g each
- 2 eggs, beaten
- ¼ cup milk
- 1 cup all-purpose flour
- 1 tbsp paprika
- ½ tsp white pepper
- vegetable oil, for frying
- salt and pepper

GRAVY

- 4 oz/115 g ground pork sausage, or pork sausage link with casing removed
- 3 scallions, white parts chopped, green parts sliced
- 3 tbsp butter
- ¼ cup all-purpose flour
- 2½ cups milk
- pinch of cayenne pepper
- salt and pepper

1 Generously season both sides of the steaks with salt and black pepper.

2 Whisk together the eggs and milk in a pie pan and reserve. Add the flour, paprika, and white pepper to a second pie pan, and mix well to combine.

3 One at a time, dip the steaks into the egg mixture, turning to coat completely, and then dredge in the flour, coating both sides. Place the egged-and-floured steaks on a plate, and let rest for 10 minutes.

4 Add about ¼ inch/5 mm of oil to a large skillet, and place over medium–high heat. When the oil begins to shimmer, add the steaks and cook for about 3–4 minutes on each side, until golden brown and cooked through.

5 Remove and drain on a wire rack set over some paper towels. If working in batches, keep the cooked steaks warm until the rest are cooked.

6 To make the gravy, lightly brown the sausage in a medium saucepan over medium heat. As it cooks, break up the meat into very small pieces with a wooden spoon. Add the white parts of the scallions and the butter and sauté for a few minutes, until the scallions are translucent.

7 Stir in the flour and cook the mixture for 3 minutes. Gradually whisk in the milk until combined. The gravy will thicken as it heats. When it simmers, reduce the heat to low and cook, stirring occasionally, for an additional 15 minutes. Add the cayenne pepper and season with salt and pepper to taste. Pour the gravy over the steaks and garnish with the sliced green scallion tops.

GRANDMOTHER'S TIP
The thickness of this gravy is easily adjusted by adding another splash of milk toward the end of the cooking process.

Johnnycakes

MAKES 12 CAKES

INGREDIENTS

- 1 cup yellow cornmeal
- 1 tbsp salt
- 1 tbsp sugar
- 1 cup boiling water
- 4 tbsp reserved bacon drippings or sunflower oil, for frying
- butter and maple syrup or honey, to serve

1 Preheat the oven to 225°F/110°C and line a heatproof plate with paper towels. Put the cornmeal, salt, and sugar into a large bowl and stir. Add ¾ cup of the water and stir to make a thick batter. Gradually stir in enough of the remaining water to make a smooth batter that drops from the spoon. If the batter is too thin, the cakes will fall apart when you turn them over.

2 Heat a large, heavy-bottom skillet over high heat until very hot. Melt the drippings in the skillet and swirl around, then pour it into a small heatproof bowl.

3 Drop 2 tablespoons of the batter into the skillet and flatten each into a 3-inch/7.5-cm circle about ¼ inch/5 mm thick. Add as many more cakes as will fit without overcrowding the skillet. Fry for 1½ minutes, or until golden brown and set underneath. Turn over and continue frying for an additional 1–2 minutes, until golden.

4 Transfer the cooked cakes to the prepared plate and keep warm while frying the remaining batter, adding more bacon drippings to the skillet as required. Serve hot with butter and maple syrup.

GRANDMOTHER'S TIP
In Vermont, Rhode Island, and other New England states, johnnycakes are traditionally made with white cornmeal.

Icebox Cookies

MAKES ABOUT 56 COOKIES
INGREDIENTS

- 2⅓ cups all-purpose flour
- 2 tbsp unsweetened cocoa
- ½ tsp baking soda
- 1 tsp ground ginger
- ½ tsp ground cinnamon
- ½ cup molasses
- 4 tbsp boiling water
- ½ cup butter, softened
- 4 tbsp superfine sugar
- confectioners' sugar, for dusting

1 Sift the flour, cocoa, baking soda, ginger, and cinnamon together into a bowl, then set aside. Mix the molasses with the water and set aside.

2 Put the butter into a large bowl and beat with an electric mixer until creamy. Slowly add the superfine sugar and continue beating until light and fluffy. Gradually add the flour mixture, alternating it with the molasses mixture to form a soft dough.

3 Scrape equal amounts of the dough onto two pieces of plastic wrap and roll into logs, using the plastic wrap as a guide, each about 7½ inches/19 cm long and 1½ inches/4 cm thick. Put the dough logs in the refrigerator for 2 hours, then transfer to the freezer for at least 2 hours and up to 2 months.

4 When ready to bake, preheat the oven to 350°F/180°C and line one or two cookie sheets, depending on how many cookies you are baking, with nonstick parchment paper. Unwrap the dough, trim the ends, and cut off ¼-inch/5 mm slices. Rewrap any unused dough and return to the freezer.

5 Place the dough slices on the prepared cookie sheet(s) and bake in the preheated oven for 12 minutes. Let cool on the cookie sheet(s) for 3 minutes, then transfer to wire racks, dust with confectioner's sugar, and let cool completely.

GRANDMOTHER'S TIP
If you like perfectly round cookies, stand the dough upright in a tall glass while chilling in step 3. Remove from the glass before transferring to the freezer.

Gelatin Dessert

SERVES 4

INGREDIENTS

- 2 envelopes orange-
  flavored gelatin powder,
  4 oz/115 g each
- 2 cups boiling water
- 1½ cups pomegranate juice
- ½ cup sour cream, beaten
- 5 tbsp pomegranate seeds,
  plus extra to decorate
- ½ cup finely diced mango

FRUIT SALAD

- 5 oz/140 g canned
  mandarin orange segments
  in juice, drained
- 1 cup drained and chopped
  pineapple chunks in juice
- ½ cup finely diced mango

1 Rinse a 3-cup/700-ml jelly mold, or four individual jelly molds, with cold water but do not dry. Put the gelatin in a heatproof bowl, add the boiling water, and stir until the gelatin is dissolved. Whisk the pomegranate juice and sour cream together until the cream is blended into the juice, then stir into the gelatin.

2 Pour the mixture into a bowl and let cool, then chill in the refrigerator for 45 minutes, or until the gelatin is just beginning to set. Stir in the pomegranate seeds and mango, then return the mold to the refrigerator for at least 1½ hours, or until set.

3 Meanwhile, to make the fruit salad, mix the orange segments, pineapple, and mango together. Cover and let chill in the refrigerator until required.

4 When ready to serve, place a plate on top of the mold, then invert the plate and mold, giving a sharp shake. Carefully lift off the mold. Spoon the fruit salad around the gelatin and sprinkle extra pomegranate seeds over. Serve immediately or return to the refrigerator until required.

GRANDMOTHER'S TIP
If you can't find pomegranate juice, you could replace it with another fruit juice. Don't use pineapple juice, though, as this will prevent the gelatin from setting properly.

Apple Pie

SERVES 6

INGREDIENTS

PIE DOUGH

- 2½ cups all-purpose flour, plus extra for dusting
- pinch of salt
- 6 tbsp butter, cut into small pieces, plus extra for greasing
- 6 tbsp lard or vegetable shortening, cut into small pieces
- about 6 tbsp cold water
- beaten egg or milk, for glazing

FILLING

- 1 lb 10 oz–2 lb 4 oz/ 750 g–1 kg baking apples, peeled, cored, and sliced
- scant ⅔ cup brown or superfine sugar, plus extra for sprinkling
- ½–1 tsp ground cinnamon, allspice, or ground ginger
- 1–2 tbsp water (optional)

1 To make the pie dough, sift the flour and salt into a large bowl. Add the butter and lard and rub in with your fingertips until the mixture resembles fine breadcrumbs. Add the water and gather the mixture together into a dough. Wrap the dough and let chill in the refrigerator for 30 minutes.

2 Preheat the oven to 425°F/220°C. Turn out almost two-thirds of the pie dough onto a floured counter, roll out thinly, and use to line a deep 9-inch/23-cm pie plate or pie pan.

3 To make the filling, mix the apples with the sugar and spice and pack into the pastry shell. Add the water, if needed, particularly if the apples are a dry variety.

4 Roll out the remaining pie dough to form a lid. Dampen the edges of the pie rim with water and position the lid, pressing the edges firmly together. Trim and crimp the edges.

5 Use the trimmings to cut out leaves or other shapes to decorate the top of the pie. Dampen and attach. Glaze the top of the pie with beaten egg, make 1–2 slits in the top, and place the pie on a baking sheet.

6 Bake in the preheated oven for 20 minutes, then reduce the oven temperature to 350°F/180°C and bake for an additional 30 minutes, or until the pastry is golden brown. Serve hot or cold, sprinkled with sugar.

GRANDMOTHER'S TIP
Prevent apples from discoloring by placing the peeled slices in a bowl of water with the juice of 1 lemon added.

Popovers

MAKES 6 POPOVERS
INGREDIENTS

- 2 tbsp beef drippings or sunflower oil
- 1 cup all-purpose flour
- ½ tsp salt
- 2 extra-large eggs
- 1 cup milk

1 Grease six metal popover molds or six cups in a muffin pan with the drippings, then divide the remaining drippings between the molds. Preheat the oven to 425°F/220°C, placing the molds in the oven so the drippings can melt while the oven heats.

2 Sift the flour and salt together into a large mixing bowl and make a well in the center. Break the eggs into the well, add the milk, and beat, gradually drawing in the flour from the side to make a smooth batter. Remove the molds from the oven and spoon in the batter until they are about halfway full.

3 Bake in the preheated oven for 30–35 minutes, without opening the door, until the popovers are well risen, puffed, and golden brown. Serve immediately.

GRANDMOTHER'S TIP
Provide each child with a money box to start a savings habit. Let them keep whatever they find during regular coin hunts down the back of the couch and under furniture.

Scones

MAKES 10–12 SCONES

INGREDIENTS

- 3⅔ cups all-purpose flour, plus extra for dusting
- ½ tsp salt
- 2 tsp baking powder
- 4 tbsp butter
- 2 tbsp superfine sugar
- 1¼ cups milk
- Classic Strawberry Jelly (see page 38) and whipped cream, to serve

1 Preheat the oven to 425°F/220°C.

2 Sift the flour, salt, and baking powder into a bowl. Rub in the butter until the mixture resembles breadcrumbs. Stir in the sugar.

3 Make a well in the center, reserve 3 tablespoons of the milk, and pour in the remaining milk. Stir in, using a round-blade knife, and make a soft dough.

4 Turn out the mixture onto a floured counter and very lightly flatten the dough until it is of an even thickness, about ½ inch/1 cm.

5 Use a 2½-inch/6-cm cookie cutter to cut out the scones and place on a baking sheet.

6 Brush the scones with the reserved milk and bake in the preheated oven for 10–12 minutes, until golden and well risen.

7 Remove from the oven and let cool on a wire rack. Serve freshly baked with Strawberry Jelly and cream.

GRANDMOTHER'S TIP
To make fruit scones, add 1/3 cup dried fruit with the sugar. To make whole wheat scones, use whole wheat flour and omit the sugar.

Classic Strawberry Jelly

MAKES ABOUT 1½ CUPS

INGREDIENTS

- 3 lb 5 oz/1.5 kg ripe, unblemished whole strawberries, hulled and rinsed
- 2 freshly squeezed lemons, juice strained
- 7½ cups sugar
- 1 tsp butter

1 Place the strawberries in a large pan with the lemon juice, then simmer over gentle heat for 15–20 minutes, stirring occasionally, until the fruit has collapsed and is very soft.

2 Add the sugar and heat, stirring occasionally, until the sugar has completely dissolved. Add the butter, then bring to a boil and boil rapidly for 10–20 minutes, or until the setting point is reached.

3 Let cool for 8–10 minutes, then skim. Put into warmed sterilized jars and cover the tops with wax disks. When completely cold, cover with cellophane or lids, then label and store in a cool place.

GRANDMOTHER'S TIP
Other flavors can be added if you like. Add 2 lightly bruised lemongrass stalks and 4 lightly bruised green cardamom pods. Discard the spices before canning.

Orange & Squash Marmalade

MAKES ABOUT 7 CUPS

INGREDIENTS

- 7 cups cubed acorn or butternut squash
- 6 blood oranges, scrubbed
- ⅔ cup freshly squeezed lemon juice
- small piece fresh ginger, peeled and grated
- 2 serrano chiles, seeded and finely sliced
- 5 cups water
- 6¼ cups sugar

1 Place the squash in a large pan with a tight-fitting lid. Thinly slice two of the oranges without peeling, reserving the seeds, and add to the pan. Peel the remaining oranges and chop the flesh, then add to the pan together with the lemon juice, ginger, and chiles. Tie up the orange seeds in a piece of cheesecloth and add to the pan with the water.

2 Bring to a boil. Reduce the heat, then cover and simmer gently for 1 hour, or until the squash and oranges are very soft. Remove the seeds and discard.

3 Add the sugar and heat gently, stirring, until the sugar has completely dissolved. Bring to a boil and boil rapidly for 15 minutes, or until the setting point is reached.

4 Skim, if necessary, then let cool for 10 minutes. Put into warmed sterilized jars and cover the tops with wax disks. When completely cold, cover with cellophane or lids, then label and store in a cool place.

GRANDMOTHER'S TIP
This marmalade is ideal for serving with meat and cheese dishes. The marmalade can also be served warm. Heat gently before serving.

Traditional Lemon Curd

MAKES ABOUT 2¾ CUPS

INGREDIENTS

- 4 lemons (preferably unwaxed and organic), scrubbed and dried
- 4 eggs, beaten
- ½ cup unsalted butter, diced
- 2¼ cups sugar

1 Finely grate the rind from the lemons and squeeze out all the juice. Place the rind and juice in a heatproof bowl, then stir in the eggs and add the butter and sugar.

2 Place over a saucepan of gently simmering water, ensuring that the bottom of the bowl does not touch the water. Cook, stirring continuously, until the sugar has completely dissolved, then continue to cook, stirring frequently, until the mixture thickens and coats the back of the spoon.

3 Spoon into warmed sterilized jars and cover the tops with wax disks. When completely cold, cover with cellophane or lids, then label and store in a cool, dark place. Use within 3 months and, once opened, store in the refrigerator.

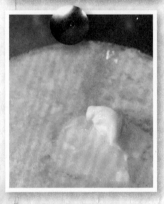

GRANDMOTHER'S TIP
Other fruits can be used in this recipe. Try orange or lime or even a mixture of all three. Add the flesh and seeds of a ripe passion fruit to the mixture when adding the sugar.

OLD-FASHIONED FOOD COMFORTS

Tomato Soup

SERVES 4

INGREDIENTS

- 4 tbsp butter
- 1 onion, finely chopped
- 3¾ cups finely chopped tomatoes
- 2½ cups hot chicken stock or vegetable stock
- pinch of sugar
- 2 tbsp shredded fresh basil leaves, plus extra sprigs to garnish
- 1 tbsp chopped fresh parsley
- salt and pepper
- croutons, to serve (optional)

1 Melt half of the butter in a large, heavy-bottom saucepan. Add the onion and cook over low heat, stirring occasionally, for 5 minutes, or until softened. Add the tomatoes, season with salt and pepper to taste, and cook for 5 minutes.

2 Pour in the stock, return to a boil, then reduce the heat and cook for 10 minutes.

3 Push the soup through a strainer with the back of a wooden spoon to remove the tomato skins and seeds. Return to the pan and stir in the sugar, remaining butter, basil, and parsley. Heat through briefly, but do not let boil.

4 Ladle into warmed soup bowls. Serve immediately, garnished with sprigs of basil and accompanied by croutons, if using.

HEART WARMING FOOD

Split Pea & Ham Soup

SERVES 6–8
INGREDIENTS

- 2½ cups split green peas
- 1 tbsp olive oil
- 1 large onion, finely chopped
- 1 large carrot, finely chopped
- 1 celery stalk, finely chopped
- 4 cups chicken stock or vegetable stock
- 4 cups water
- 8 oz/225 g lean smoked ham, finely diced
- ¼ tsp dried thyme
- ¼ tsp dried marjoram
- 1 bay leaf
- salt and pepper

1 Rinse the peas under cold running water. Put in a saucepan and cover generously with water. Bring to a boil and boil for 3 minutes, skimming off the foam from the surface. Drain the peas.

2 Heat the oil in a large saucepan over medium heat. Add the onion and cook for 3–4 minutes, stirring occasionally, until just softened. Add the carrot and celery and cook for 2 minutes.

3 Add the peas, pour over the stock and water, and stir to combine. Bring just to a boil and stir the ham into the soup. Add the thyme, marjoram, and bay leaf. Reduce the heat, cover, and cook gently for 1–1½ hours, until the ingredients are very soft. Remove and discard the bay leaf.

4 Taste and adjust the seasoning, then ladle into warmed soup bowls and serve.

Hearty Beef Stew

SERVES 4

INGREDIENTS

- 3 lb/1.3 kg boneless chuck roast, cut into 2-inch/5-cm pieces
- 2 tbsp vegetable oil
- 2 yellow onions, cut into 1-inch/2.5-cm pieces
- 3 tbsp flour
- 3 garlic cloves, finely chopped
- 4 cups cold beef stock or broth
- 3 carrots, peeled and cut into 1-inch/2.5-cm pieces
- 2 celery stalks, cut into 1-inch/2.5-cm pieces
- 1 tbsp ketchup
- 1 bay leaf
- ¼ tsp dried rosemary
- ¼ tsp dried thyme
- 1 tsp salt
- 2 lb/900 g Yukon gold potatoes, peeled and cut into large chunks
- salt and pepper
- fresh flat-leaf parsley, to garnish

1 Season the beef very generously with salt and pepper. Add the oil to a large, heavy-bottom saucepan or Dutch oven (one that has a tight-fitting lid), and set over high heat. When the oil begins to smoke slightly, add the beef and brown very well. Work in batches if necessary. Once well-browned, transfer the beef to a bowl using a slotted spoon, leaving the oil and beef drippings in the pan.

2 Reduce the heat to medium, add the onions to the pan, and sauté for about 5 minutes, or until translucent. Add the flour and cook for 2 minutes, stirring frequently. Add the garlic and cook for 1 minute. Whisk in 1 cup of the stock to deglaze the bottom of the pan, scraping up any sediment.

3 Add the remaining broth, carrots, celery, ketchup, bay leaf, rosemary, thyme, beef, and salt. Bring back to a gentle simmer, cover, and cook over low heat for 1 hour. Add the potatoes and simmer, covered, for an additonal 30 minutes. Remove the cover, increase the heat to medium, and cook, stirring occasionally, for an additional 30 minutes, or until the meat and vegetables are tender.

4 This final 30 minutes of cooking will reduce and thicken the sauce. If the stew gets too thick, add some more stock or water. Turn off the heat, taste, and adjust the seasoning, then let sit for 15 minutes before serving. Garnish with parsley, if using.

GRANDMOTHER'S TIP
Braising beef is a term used for several cuts of beef that are suited to long, slow cooking. Look for a marbling of fat through the meat, which will break down during cooking and add flavor.

Hot Dogs & Mashed Potatoes

SERVES 4

INGREDIENTS

- 1 tbsp olive oil
- 8 good-quality hot dogs

ONION GRAVY
- 3 onions, halved and thinly sliced
- 5 tbsp butter
- ½ cup Marsala or port
- ½ cup vegetable stock
- salt and pepper

MASHED POTATOES
- 2 lb/900 g floury potatoes, such as russet potatoes, peeled and cut into chunks
- 4 tbsp butter
- 3 tbsp hot milk
- 2 tbsp chopped fresh parsley

1 Place a skillet over low heat, then add oil and the hot dogs. Cover and cook for 25–30 minutes, turning the hot dogs from time to time, until browned all over.

2 Meanwhile, prepare the onion gravy by placing the onions in a skillet with the butter and frying over low heat until softened, stirring continuously. Continue to cook for around 30 minutes, or until the onions are browned and have started to caramelize.

3 Pour in the Marsala and stock and continue to simmer until the onion gravy is really thick. Season with salt and pepper to taste.

4 To make the mashed potatoes, bring a large saucepan of lightly salted water to a boil, add the potatoes, and cook for 15–20 minutes. Drain well and mash with a potato masher until smooth. Season with salt and pepper to taste, add the butter, milk, and parsley, and stir well.

5 Serve the hot dogs immediately with the mashed potatoes and the onion gravy spooned over the top.

GRANDMOTHER'S TIP
When cooking lots of hot dogs under the broiler or on a grill thread them on to skewers. This will make them easy to turn.

Steak Sandwiches

SERVES 4

INGREDIENTS

- 8 slices thick white bread or whole wheat bread
- butter, for spreading
- 2 handfuls of mixed salad greens
- 3 tbsp olive oil
- 2 onions, thinly sliced
- 1 lb 8 oz/675 g sirloin or top round steak, about 1-inch/2.5-cm thick
- 1 tbsp Worcestershire sauce
- 2 tbsp whole-grain mustard
- 2 tbsp water
- salt and pepper

1 Spread each slice of bread with some butter and add a few salad greens to the bottom slices.

2 Heat 2 tablespoons of the oil in a large, heavy-bottom skillet over medium heat. Add the onions and cook, stirring occasionally, for 10–15 minutes, until softened and golden brown. Using a slotted spoon, transfer to a plate and set aside.

3 Increase the heat to high and add the remaining oil to the skillet. Add the steak, season with pepper to taste, and cook quickly on both sides to seal. Reduce the heat to medium and cook, turning once, for 2½–3 minutes each side for rare or 3½–5 minutes each side for medium. Transfer the steak to a plate.

4 Add the Worcestershire sauce, mustard, and water to the skillet and stir to deglaze by scraping any sediment from the bottom of the skillet. Return the onions to the skillet, season with salt and pepper to taste, and mix well.

5 Thinly slice the steak across the grain, divide it among the 4 bottom slices of bread, and cover with the onions. Cover with the top halves of bread and press down gently. Serve immediately.

FEEL-BETTER FOOD

Ham & Cheese Sandwich

MAKES I SANDWICH
INGREDIENTS

- 2 slices country-style bread,
  such as white Italian bread,
  thinly sliced
- 4 tsp butter,
  at room temperature
- ½ cup grated
  Gruyère cheese
- I slice cooked ham,
  trimmed to fit the bread,
  if necessary
- potato chips,
  to serve (optional)

1 Thinly spread each slice of bread on I side with butter, then put I slice on the counter, buttered side down. Sprinkle over half of the cheese, taking it to the edge of the bread, then add the ham and top with the remaining cheese. Add the other slice of bread, buttered-side up, and press down.

2 Heat a heavy-bottom skillet, ideally nonstick, over medium–high heat until hot. Reduce the heat to medium, add the sandwich, and fry on one side for 2–3 minutes, until golden brown.

3 Flip the sandwich over and fry on the other side for 2–3 minutes, until all the cheese is melted and the bread is golden brown. Cut in half diagonally and serve immediately with potato chips on the side, if using.

QUICK AND
SIMPLE FIX

Tuna Melts

MAKES 4 MELTS
INGREDIENTS

- 4 slices sourdough bread
- 14 oz/400 g canned tuna, drained and flaked
- 4 tbsp mayonnaise, or to taste
- 1 tbsp Dijon mustard or whole grain mustard, plus extra, to taste
- 4 scallions, trimmed and chopped
- 2 tbsp finely chopped dill pickle or sweet pickle, to taste
- 1 hard-cooked egg, shelled and finely chopped
- 1 small carrot, grated
- 1 tbsp rinsed and coarsely chopped capers in brine
- 2 tbsp chopped parsley or chives
- 4 large lettuce leaves, such as romaine
- 8 thin slices cheddar cheese
- salt and pepper

1 Preheat the broiler to high and position the broiler rack about 4 inches/10 cm from the heat source. Line a cookie sheet with foil and set aside. Toast the bread under the preheated broiler for 2 minutes on each side, or until crisp and lightly browned.

2 Meanwhile, put the tuna in a bowl with the mayonnaise and mustard and beat together to break up the tuna. Add the scallions, pickle, egg, carrot, capers, and salt and pepper to taste and beat together, adding extra mayonnaise to taste. Stir in the parsley.

3 Put the toast on the foil-lined baking sheet and top each slice with a lettuce leaf. Divide the tuna salad among the slices of toast and spread out. Top each sandwich with cheese slices, cut to fit.

4 Place under the broiler and broil for 2 minutes, or until the cheese is melted and very lightly browned. Cut each tuna melt into four slices, transfer to a plate, and serve immediately.

Pasta with Pesto

SERVES 4

INGREDIENTS

- 1 lb/450 g dried tagliatelle
- fresh basil sprigs, to garnish

PESTO
- 2 garlic cloves
- ¼ cup pine nuts
- 2½ cups fresh basil leaves
- ½ cup freshly grated Parmesan cheese
- ½ cup olive oil
- salt

1 To make the pesto, put the garlic, pine nuts, a large pinch of salt, and the basil into a mortar, and pound to a paste with a pestle. Transfer to a bowl and gradually work in the cheese with a wooden spoon, followed by the olive oil, to make a thick, creamy sauce. Taste and adjust the seasoning, if necessary.

2 Alternatively, put the garlic, pine nuts, and a large pinch of salt into a food processor or blender and process briefly. Add the basil leaves and process to a paste. With the motor still running, gradually add the olive oil. Scrape into a bowl and beat in the cheese. Season with salt to taste.

3 Bring a large saucepan of lightly salted water to a boil. Add the pasta, return to a boil, and cook for 8–10 minutes, or according to the package directions, until tender but still firm to the bite.

4 Drain the pasta well, return to the pan, and toss with half of the pesto, then divide among warmed serving plates and top with the remaining pesto. Garnish with basil sprigs and serve immediately.

GRANDMOTHER'S TIP
Try replacing the tomato sauce on your homemade pizza with pesto, top with mozzarella cheese, and bake.

Macaroni & Cheese

SERVES 4

INGREDIENTS

- 9 oz/250 g dried macaroni
- 4 tbsp butter, plus extra for cooking the pasta
- 2½ cups milk
- ½ tsp grated nutmeg
- scant ½ cup all-purpose flour
- ¾ cup grated sharp cheddar cheese
- ¾ cup grated Parmesan cheese
- 7 oz/200 g baby spinach
- salt and pepper

1 Cook the macaroni according to the package directions. Remove from the heat, drain, add a small pat of butter to keep it soft, return to the saucepan, and cover to keep warm.

2 Put the milk and nutmeg into a separate saucepan over low heat and heat until warm, but don't boil. Melt the butter in a heavy-bottom saucepan over low heat, add the flour, and stir to make a roux. Cook gently for 2 minutes. Add the milk a little at a time, whisking it into the roux, then cook for 10–15 minutes to make a loose sauce.

3 Add three-quarters of the cheddar cheese and Parmesan cheese and stir through until they have melted in, then add the spinach, season with salt and pepper, and remove from the heat.

4 Preheat the broiler to high. Put the macaroni into a shallow heatproof dish, then pour the sauce over. Scatter the remaining cheeses over the top and place the dish under the preheated broiler. Broil until the cheeses begin to brown, then serve.

GRANDMOTHER'S TIP
You can add texture to this by sprinkling some whole wheat breadcrumbs over the cheese before placing under the broiler.

Tuna & Pasta Casserole

SERVES 4–6

INGREDIENTS

- 7 oz/200 g dried ribbon egg pasta, such as tagliatelle
- 2 tbsp butter
- 1 cup fine fresh breadcrumbs
- 14 fl oz/400 ml canned condensed cream of mushroom soup
- ½ cup milk
- 2 celery stalks, chopped
- 1 red bell pepper, seeded and chopped
- 1 green bell pepper, seeded and chopped
- 1¼ cups coarsely grated sharp cheddar cheese
- 2 tbsp chopped fresh parsley
- 7 oz/200 g canned tuna in oil, drained and flaked
- salt and pepper

1 Preheat the oven to 400°F/200°C. Bring a large saucepan of lightly salted water to a boil. Add the pasta, return to a boil, and cook for 2 minutes less than specified on the package directions.

2 Meanwhile, melt the butter in a separate small saucepan. Stir in the breadcrumbs, then remove from the heat and set aside.

3 Drain the pasta well and set aside. Pour the soup into the pasta pan over medium heat, then stir in the milk, celery, bell peppers, half of the cheese, and all the parsley. Add the tuna and gently stir in so that the flakes don't break up. Season with salt and pepper to taste. Heat just until small bubbles appear around the edge of the mixture—do not boil.

4 Stir the pasta into the pan and use two forks to mix all the ingredients together. Spoon the mixture into an ovenproof dish that is also suitable for serving, and spread it out.

5 Stir the remaining cheese into the buttered breadcrumbs, then sprinkle over the top of the pasta mixture. Bake in the preheated oven for 20–25 minutes, or until the topping is golden. Remove from the oven, then let stand for 5 minutes before serving straight from the dish.

DELICIOUS & ECONOMICAL

Cauliflower Cheese Gratin

SERVES 4

INGREDIENTS

- 1 head of cauliflower, trimmed and cut into florets
- 3 tbsp butter
- ⅓ cup all-purpose flour
- 2 cups milk
- 1 cup finely grated cheddar cheese,
- whole nutmeg, for grating
- 1 tbsp grated Parmesan cheese
- salt and pepper

1 Bring a saucepan of lightly salted water to a boil, add the cauliflower florets, and cook for 4–5 minutes. They should still be firm. Drain, place in a warmed 1½-quart/1.4-liter gratin dish, and keep warm.

2 Melt the butter in the rinsed-out saucepan over medium heat and stir in the flour. Cook for 1 minute, stirring continuously.

3 Remove from the heat and gradually stir in the milk until the sauce has achieved a smooth consistency.

4 Return to low heat and continue to stir while the sauce comes to a boil and thickens. Reduce the heat and simmer gently, stirring continuously, for about 3 minutes, until the sauce is creamy and smooth.

5 Remove from the heat and stir in the cheddar cheese and a good grating of the nutmeg. Taste and season well with salt and pepper.

6 Pour the hot sauce over the cauliflower, top with the Parmesan cheese, and place under a hot broiler to brown. Serve immediately.

GRANDMOTHER'S TIP
Using a mixture of cauliflower and broccoli will give a more colorful dish. You can make it even more substantial by adding some fried sliced onions and fried bacon pieces before pouring over the sauce.

Salmon-Stuffed Potatoes

SERVES 4

INGREDIENTS

- 4 baking potatoes, about 9¾ oz/275 g each, scrubbed
- 9 oz/250 g skinless salmon fillet
- 7 oz/200 g low-fat soft cheese
- 2–3 tbsp skim milk
- 2 tbsp chopped/snipped fresh herbs, such as dill or chives
- generous ½ cup grated sharp cheddar cheese
- salt and pepper

1 Preheat the oven to 400°F/200°C. Prick the skins of the potatoes and put on the top shelf of the preheated oven. Bake for 50–60 minutes, or until the skins are crisp and the centers are soft when pierced with a sharp knife or skewer.

2 Meanwhile, lightly poach the salmon fillet in a saucepan of gently simmering water for 4–5 minutes (if in one piece), or until just cooked but still moist. Alternatively, cut into 2–3 equal pieces and cook in a microwave oven on medium heat for 2 minutes, then turn the pieces around so that the cooked parts are in the center and cook for an additional 1 minute, or until just cooked but still moist. Using a fork, flake the flesh into a bowl.

3 In a separate bowl, blend the soft cheese with just enough of the milk to loosen, then stir in the herbs and a little salt and pepper.

4 When the potatoes are cooked, preheat the broiler to high. Cut the potatoes in half lengthwise. Carefully scoop the potato flesh out of the skins, reserving the skins, then add to the soft cheese mixture and mash together. Lightly stir in the salmon flakes.

5 Spoon the filling into the potato skins and top with the cheddar cheese. Cook under the preheated broiler for 1–2 minutes, or until the cheese is bubbling and turning golden. Serve immediately.

GRANDMOTHER'S TIP
Ensure the potatoes are baked through so that they're soft inside and the skins are firm and crisp, which makes them very delicious. You can even rub salt and oil into the skins to enhance the flavor.

Chicken Pot Pie

SERVES 6

INGREDIENTS

- 1 tbsp olive oil
- 3¼ cups sliced white button mushrooms
- 1 onion, finely chopped
- 2 cups sliced carrots
- 1 cup sliced celery
- 4 cups cold chicken broth
- 6 tbsp butter
- ½ cup all-purpose flour, plus extra for dusting
- 2 lb/900 g skinless, boneless chicken breasts, cut into 1-inch/2.5-cm cubes
- 1 cup frozen peas
- 1 tsp chopped fresh thyme leaves or a pinch of dried thyme
- 1 tsp salt
- ¼ tsp pepper
- 2½ quantities Pie Dough (see page 186) or 1lb 8 oz/ 675 g prepared pastry
- 1 egg, beaten

1 Heat the oil in a large saucepan, add the mushrooms and onion, and sauté over medium heat until golden. Add the carrots, celery, and 2 cups of the broth. Bring to a boil, reduce the heat to low, and simmer until the vegetables are almost tender.

2 Melt the butter in a large saucepan over medium heat. Whisk in the flour and cook, stirring, for 4 minutes, or until the flour is a light tan color and smells like cooked piecrust. Slowly whisk in the remaining broth. Simmer, stirring, over medium–low heat until the mixture thickens. Remove from the heat and reserve.

3 Add the vegetables and broth from the other pan to the flour mixture when ready, and stir to combine. Add the chicken, peas, thyme, salt, and pepper. Return to a simmer and cook, stirring, for 5 minutes. Taste for seasoning and set aside until needed.

4 Preheat the oven to 400°F/200°C. Divide the pot pie filling among 6 large ramekins, filling up to ½ inch/ 1 cm from the top).

5 Cut out circles of pie dough 1 inch/2.5 cm larger than the diameter of the ramekins. Place the dough over the pot pies. Go around each piece of dough, folding ½ inch/ 1 cm over to form a rim. Pinch with your fingertips to form a crimped edge. Cut a small cross in the center of each.

6 Place the ramekins on a baking sheet. Brush the tops with the beaten egg. Bake in the preheated oven for 35–40 minutes, or until the pies are golden brown and bubbly. Let cool for 15 minutes before serving.

GRANDMOTHER'S TIP
To thaw pastry quickly, separate the sheets and cover each one in plastic wrap, then let thaw at room temperature for 30 minutes.

Homemade Hamburgers

SERVES 6

INGREDIENTS

- 2 lb 4 oz/1 kg ground beef
- 1 small onion, grated
- 1 tbsp chopped fresh parsley
- 2 tsp Worcestershire sauce
- 2 tbsp sunflower oil
- salt and pepper

TO SERVE

- 6 hamburger buns,
  split and toasted
- salad greens
- tomato slices
- dill pickles, sliced
- ketchup

1 Put the ground beef, onion, parsley, and Worcestershire sauce into a bowl, season with salt and pepper to taste, and mix well with your hands until thoroughly combined.

2 Divide the mixture into 6 equal portions and shape each into a ball, then gently flatten into a hamburger shape. If you have time, chill in the refrigerator for 30 minutes to firm up.

3 Heat the oil in a large skillet. Add the hamburgers, in batches, and cook over medium heat for 5–8 minutes on each side, turning them carefully with a spatula. Remove from the skillet and keep warm while you cook the remaining hamburgers.

4 Serve in toasted hamburger buns with salad greens, tomato slices, dill pickles, and ketchup.

GUILTY PLEASURE

GRANDMOTHER'S TIP
Make a large batch of hamburgers and freeze, stored in a plastic container with wax paper between the hamburgers to keep them separate.

Traditional Pizza

SERVES 6

INGREDIENTS

PIZZA DOUGH
- ½ oz/15 g active dry yeast
- 1 tsp sugar
- 1 cup lukewarm water
- 2¾ cups white bread flour, plus extra for dusting
- 1 tsp salt
- 1 tbsp olive oil, plus extra for oiling

TOPPING
- 14 oz/400 g canned chopped tomatoes
- 2 garlic cloves, crushed
- 2 tsp dried basil
- 1 tbsp olive oil
- 2 tbsp tomato paste
- 3½ oz/100 g mozzarella cheese, chopped
- 2 tbsp freshly grated Parmesan cheese
- salt and pepper
- fresh besil leaves, to garnish

1 Place the yeast and sugar in a measuring cup and mix with 4 tbsp of the water. Let stand in a warm place for 15 minutes, or until frothy.

2 Mix the flour with the salt and make a well in the center. Add the oil, yeast mixture, and the remaining water. Using a wooden spoon, mix to form a smooth dough.

3 Turn out the dough onto a floured counter and knead for 4–5 minutes or until smooth.

4 Return the dough to the bowl, cover with an oiled sheet of plastic wrap, and let rise for 30 minutes, or until doubled in size.

5 Knead the dough for 2 minutes. Stretch the dough with a rolling pin, then place it on an oiled cookie sheet or pizza pan, pushing out the edges until even. The dough should be no more than ¼ inch/6 mm thick because it will rise during cooking.

6 Preheat the oven to 400°F/200°C. To make the topping, place the tomatoes, garlic, dried basil, olive oil, and salt and pepper to taste in a large skillet and let simmer for 20 minutes, or until the sauce has thickened. Stir in the tomato paste and let cool slightly.

7 Spread the topping evenly over the pizza crust. Top with the mozzarella cheese and Parmesan cheese and bake in the preheated oven for 20–25 minutes. Serve hot, garnished with basil leaves.

PRACTICE MAKES PERFECT

Crab Cakes with Tartare Sauce

MAKES 6 CRAB CAKES
INGREDIENTS

- 1 extra-large egg, beaten
- 2 tbsp mayonnaise
- ½ tsp Dijon mustard
- ¼ tsp Worcestershire sauce
- ½ tsp Old Bay seasoning
- ¼ tsp salt, or to taste
- pinch of cayenne pepper (optional)
- 10 saltine crackers
- 1 lb/450 g fresh crabmeat,
- ⅓–¾ cup plain breadcrumbs
- 1 tbsp vegetable oil
- 2 tbsp unsalted butter
- salad greens and lemon wedges, to serve

TARTARE SAUCE

- 1 cup mayonnaise
- ¼ cup sweet pickle relish
- 1 tbsp very finely chopped onion
- 1 tbsp chopped capers
- 1 tbsp chopped parsley
- 1½ tbsp freshly squeezed lemon juice
- dash of Worcestershire sauce
- few drops of Tabasco sauce (optional)
- salt and pepper

1 To make the tartare sauce, mix all the ingredients together in a bowl and season with salt and pepper to taste. Chill for at least an hour before serving.

2 Put the egg, mayonnaise, mustard, Worcestershire sauce, Old Bay seasoning, salt, and cayenne pepper, if using, into a mixing bowl and whisk to combine. Crush the crackers into very fine crumbs, add to the bowl, and combine. Let rest for 5 minutes.

3 Gently fold in the crabmeat and mix to combine the ingredients. Try not to mash the crab any more than necessary. Cover and chill for at least 1 hour.

4 Sprinkle breadcrumbs over a large plate until lightly covered. Shape the crab mixture into 6 even-size cakes, about 1 inch/2.5 cm thick, and place on the plate as they are formed. Lightly dust the tops of each cake with more breadcrumbs.

5 Heat the oil and butter in a large skillet over medium–high heat. When the foam from the butter begins to dissipate, carefully transfer each crab cake from the plate to the skillet.

6 Sauté the cakes for about 4 minutes per side, until golden brown. Remove from the skillet, drain on paper towels, and serve with the tartare sauce, salad greens, and lemon wedges.

DINNER PARTY WINNER

Spaghetti alla Carbonara

SERVES 4

INGREDIENTS

- 1 lb/450 g dried spaghetti
- 1 tbsp olive oil
- 8 oz/225 g rindless pancetta or lean bacon, chopped
- 4 eggs
- 5 tbsp light cream
- 2 tbsp freshly grated Parmesan cheese
- salt and pepper

1 Bring a large saucepan of lightly salted water to a boil. Add the pasta, return to a boil, and cook for 8–10 minutes, or according to the package directions, until tender but still firm to the bite.

2 Meanwhile, heat the olive oil in a heavy-bottom skillet. Add the pancetta and cook over medium heat, stirring frequently, for 8–10 minutes.

3 Beat the eggs with the cream in a small bowl and season with salt and pepper to taste. Drain the pasta and return it to the pan. Add the contents of the skillet, then add the egg mixture and half of the Parmesan cheese. Stir well, then transfer to a warmed serving dish. Serve immediately, sprinkled with the remaining cheese.

GRANDMOTHER'S TIP
Sprinkling salt over spilt red wine prevents the stain from spreading, but do not do this on a rug because you'll never remove the residue. Blot with paper towels instead.

FAVORITE FAMILY DINNERS

Roasted Rib of Beef

SERVES 8

INGREDIENTS

- olive oil
- 6 lb 8-oz/3-kg joint of well-hung rib of beef on the bone
- ½ tbsp all-purpose flour
- generous ¾ cup strong chicken stock
- generous ¾ cup red wine

ROASTED POTATOES

- 4 lb 8 oz/2 kg potatoes, peeled
- 6 tbsp sunflower oil, goose fat, or duck fat
- salt and pepper

TO SERVE

- Popovers (see page 34)
- glazed carrots
- steamed broccoli
- horseradish sauce
- mustard

1 To make the roasted potatoes, bring a large saucepan of lightly salted water to a boil, add the potatoes, return to a boil, and cook for 10 minutes. Drain the potatoes and toss them in oil and salt and pepper. Put them in a roasting pan in a single layer.

2 Preheat the oven to 425°F/220°C. Rub a generous amount of oil and salt and pepper into the beef, then place in a separate roasting pan. Transfer to the preheated oven and roast for 30 minutes.

3 Reduce the oven temperature to 325°F/160°C. Transfer the potatoes to the oven and roast with the beef for 60 minutes. Remove the beef from the oven and increase the temperature to 425°F/220°C. Transfer the beef to a warmed platter, cover with foil, and let rest for at least 30 minutes.

4 Meanwhile, make the gravy. Stir the flour into the leftover juices in the pan, add the stock and wine, then simmer over medium heat, until reduced by about half.

5 Remove the potatoes from the oven. Cut the rib bones off the beef and carve the meat. Serve with the potatoes, popovers, carrots, broccoli, horseradish sauce, and mustard.

HEART WARMING FOOD

Roasted Chicken

SERVES 6

INGREDIENTS

- 5 lb/2.25 kg chicken
- 4 tbsp butter
- 2 tbsp chopped fresh lemon thyme
- 1 lemon, quartered
- ½ cup white wine, plus extra if needed
- salt and pepper

1 Preheat the oven to 425°F/220°C.

2 Make sure the chicken is clean, wiping it inside and out using paper towels, and place in a roasting pan.

3 In a bowl, soften the butter with a fork, mix in the thyme, and season well with salt and pepper.

4 Butter the chicken all over with the herb butter, inside and out, and place the lemon pieces inside the body cavity. Pour the wine over the chicken.

5 Roast in the center of the preheated oven for 20 minutes. Reduce the temperature to 375°F/190°C and continue to roast for an additional 1¼ hours, basting frequently. Cover with foil if the skin begins to brown too much. If the pan dries out, add a little more wine or water.

6 Test that the chicken is cooked by piercing the thickest part of the leg with a sharp knife or skewer and making sure the juices run clear. Remove from the oven.

7 Remove the chicken from the roasting pan and place on a warmed serving plate, cover with foil, and let rest for 10 minutes before carving.

8 Place the roasting pan on the stove and bubble the pan juices gently over low heat until they have reduced and are thick and glossy. Season with salt and pepper to taste.

9 Serve the chicken with the pan juices.

GRANDMOTHER'S TIP
To give more depth and a touch of sweetness to the finished dish, add a generous splash of Marsala to the pan juices when reducing them.

Leg of Lamb Pot Roast

SERVES 4

INGREDIENTS

- 3 lb 8 oz/1.6 kg leg of lamb
- 3–4 fresh rosemary sprigs, plus extra to garnish
- 4 oz/115 g lean bacon slices
- 4 tbsp olive oil
- 2–3 garlic cloves, crushed
- 2 onions, sliced
- 2 carrots, sliced
- 2 celery stalks, sliced
- 1¼ cups dry white wine
- 1 tbsp tomato paste
- 1¼ cups lamb stock or chicken stock
- 3 tomatoes, peeled, quartered, and seeded
- 1 tbsp chopped fresh parsley
- 1 tbsp chopped fresh oregano or marjoram
- salt and pepper

1 Preheat the oven to 325°F/160°C. Wipe the lamb all over with paper towels, trim off any excess fat, and season with salt and pepper to taste, rubbing in well. Lay the sprigs of rosemary over the lamb, cover evenly with the bacon, and securely tie in place with kitchen string.

2 Heat the oil in a skillet, add the lamb, and fry over medium heat for 10 minutes, turning several times. Remove from the skillet.

3 Transfer the oil from the skillet to a large ovenproof casserole, add the garlic and onions, and cook for 3–4 minutes, until the onions are starting to soften. Add the carrots and celery to the skillet and cook for an additional few minutes.

4 Lay the lamb on top of the vegetables and press down to partly submerge. Pour the wine over the lamb, add the tomato paste, and let simmer for 3–4 minutes. Add the stock, tomatoes, and herbs and season with salt and pepper to taste. Return to a boil for an additional 3–4 minutes.

5 Lightly cover the casserole and cook in the preheated oven for 2–2½ hours, until very tender.

6 Remove the lamb from the casserole and, if you like, remove the bacon and herbs together with the string. Keep the lamb warm. Strain the juices, skimming off any excess fat, and serve in a pitcher. The vegetables may be served around the joint or in a warmed dish. Garnish with rosemary sprigs.

IDEAL WINTER WARMER

Baked Ham

SERVES 6

INGREDIENTS

- 3 lb/1.3 kg boneless ham, presoaked if necessary
- 2 tbsp Dijon mustard
- scant ½ cup raw brown sugar
- ½ tsp ground cinnamon
- ½ tsp ground ginger
- 18 whole cloves
- orange-red currant sauce, to serve

1 Place the ham in a large saucepan, cover with cold water, and slowly bring to a boil over gentle heat. Cover and simmer very gently for 1 hour.

2 Preheat the oven to 400°F/200°C.

3 Remove the ham from the pan and drain. Remove the rind from the ham and discard. Score the fat into a diamond-shape pattern with a sharp knife.

4 Spread the mustard over the fat. Mix together the sugar and the spices on a plate and roll the ham in the mixture, pressing down well to coat evenly.

5 Stud the diamond shapes with cloves and place the ham in a roasting pan. Roast in the preheated oven for 20 minutes, until the glaze has turned a rich golden colour.

6 To serve hot, let stand for 20 minutes before carving. If the ham is to be served cold, it can be cooked a day ahead. Serve with the orange-red currant sauce.

FEEL-BETTER FOOD

GRANDMOTHER'S TIP
Stock an emergency shelf, out of the reach of children, with candles, matches, flashlights, first-aid kit, and a list of emergency telephone numbers.

Steak & French Fries

SERVES 4

INGREDIENTS

- 4 porterhouse steaks, about 8 oz/225 g each
- 4 tsp Tabasco sauce
- salt and pepper

FRENCH FRIES
- 2 large potatoes (about 1 lb/450 g), peeled
- 2 tbsp sunflower oil

WATERCRESS BUTTER
- 1 bunch of watercress
- 6 tbsp unsalted butter, softened

1 To make the French fries, preheat the oven to 400°F/ 200°C. Cut the potatoes lengthwise into thick, even fries. Rinse them under cold running water and then dry well on a clean dish towel. Place in a bowl, add the oil, and toss together until coated.

2 Spread the fries on a baking sheet and cook in the preheated oven for 40–45 minutes, turning once, until golden.

3 To make the watercress butter, finely chop enough watercress to fill ¼ cup. Place the butter in a small bowl and beat in the chopped watercress with a fork until fully incorporated. Cover with plastic wrap and let chill in the refrigerator until required.

4 Preheat a ridged grill pan to high. Sprinkle each steak with 1 teaspoon of the Tabasco sauce, rubbing it in well. Season with salt and pepper to taste.

5 Cook the steaks in the preheated pan for 2½ minutes each side for rare, 4 minutes each side for medium, and 6 minutes each side for well done. Transfer to serving plates and serve immediately, topped with the watercress butter and accompanied by the fries.

GRANDMOTHER'S TIP
To test for doneness, press the steak gently with the tip of your finger. Rare should be soft and supple, well done firm, and medium in between.

Pork Chops with Applesauce

SERVES 4

INGREDIENTS

- 4 pork rib chops on the bone, each about 1¼ inches/3 cm thick, at room temperature
- 1½ tbsp sunflower oil or canola oil
- salt and pepper

APPLESAUCE

- 4 cups peeled, cored, and diced apples, such as Gala
- 4 tbsp superfine sugar, plus extra, if needed
- finely grated zest of ½ lemon
- ½ tbsp lemon juice, plus extra, if needed
- 4 tbsp water
- ¼ tsp cinnamon
- pat of butter

1 Preheat the oven to 400°F/200°C.

2 To make the applesauce, put the apples, sugar, lemon zest, lemon juice, and water into a heavy-bottom saucepan over high heat and bring to a boil, stirring to dissolve the sugar. Reduce the heat to low, cover, and simmer for 15–20 minutes, until the apples are tender and fall apart when you mash them against the side of the pan. Stir in the cinnamon and butter and beat the apples until they are as smooth or chunky as you like. Stir in extra sugar or lemon juice, to taste. Remove the pan from the heat, cover, and keep the applesauce warm.

3 Meanwhile, pat the chops dry and season with salt and pepper to taste. Heat the oil in a large ovenproof skillet over medium–high heat. Add the chops and fry for 3 minutes on each side to brown.

4 Transfer the skillet to the preheated oven and roast the chops for 7–9 minutes, until cooked through and the juices run clear when you cut them. Remove the skillet from the oven, cover with foil, and let stand for 3 minutes. Gently reheat the applesauce, if necessary.

5 Transfer the chops to warmed plates and spoon the cooking juices over. Serve immediately, accompanied by the applesauce.

IMPRESS THE FAMILY

Barbecue-Glazed Drumsticks

SERVES 6

INGREDIENTS

- 12 chicken drumsticks
- 1 cup barbecue sauce
- 1 tbsp brown sugar
- 1 tbsp cider vinegar
- 1 tsp salt
- ½ tsp pepper
- ½ tsp hot sauce
- vegetable oil, for greasing

1 With a sharp knife, make 2 slashes, about 1 inch/ 2.5 cm apart, into the thickest part of the drumsticks, cutting to the bone. Transfer the chicken to a large, sealable plastic freezer bag.

2 In a small bowl, mix together ¼ cup of the barbecue sauce with the rest of the ingredients. Pour into the bag of chicken, press out most of the air, and seal tightly. Shake the bag gently to distribute the sauce evenly. Refrigerate for at least 4 hours.

3 Preheat the oven to 400°F/200°C. Line a baking sheet with foil and brush lightly with oil. Remove the chicken from the bag with tongs and space evenly on the prepared sheet. Discard the contents of the bag. Brush both sides of the drumsticks with some of the remaining barbecue sauce.

4 Bake in the preheated oven for 15 minutes, then remove from the oven, and brush generously with more sauce. Return to the oven, and repeat this process 3 more times for a total cooking time of 1 hour. When done, the chicken will be cooked through with a beautiful thick glaze.

CHILDREN'S FAVORITE

Fried Chicken Wings

SERVES 4

INGREDIENTS

- 12 chicken wings
- 1 egg
- ½ cup milk
- heaping 4 tbsp
  all-purpose flour
- 1 tsp paprika
- 2 cups breadcrumbs
- 4 tbsp butter
- salt and pepper

1 Preheat the oven to 425°F/220°C. Separate the chicken wings into 3 pieces each. Discard the bony tip. Beat the egg with the milk in a shallow dish. Combine the flour, paprika, and salt and pepper to taste in a separate shallow dish. Place the breadcrumbs in another shallow dish.

2 Dip the chicken pieces into the egg to coat well, then drain and roll in the seasoned flour. Remove, shaking off any excess, then roll the chicken in the breadcrumbs, gently pressing them onto the surface and shaking off any excess.

3 Put the butter in a shallow roasting pan large enough to hold all the chicken pieces in a single layer, then put in the preheated oven to melt. Remove from the oven and arrange the chicken, skin-side down, in the pan and bake in the oven for 10 minutes. Turn and bake for an additional 10 minutes, or until the chicken is tender and the juices run clear when a skewer is inserted into the thickest part of the meat.

4 Remove the chicken from the pan and arrange on a large warmed platter. Serve hot or at room temperature.

GRANDMOTHER'S TIP
It's a good idea to let coated or breaded chicken rest for about 5 minutes before cooking. This helps set the coating and bind it to the chicken.

Meat Lasagne

SERVES 6

INGREDIENTS

- 2 tbsp olive oil
- 2 oz/55 g pancetta or rindless lean bacon, chopped
- 1 onion, chopped
- 1 garlic clove, finely chopped
- 1 cup fresh ground beef
- 2 celery stalks, chopped
- 2 carrots, chopped
- pinch of sugar
- ½ tsp dried oregano
- 14 oz/400 g canned chopped tomatoes
- 8 oz/225 g dried oven-ready lasagne noodles
- 1 cup freshly grated Parmesan cheese, plus extra for sprinkling

CHEESE SAUCE

- 1¼ cups milk
- 1 bay leaf
- 6 black peppercorns
- 1 onion slice
- 1 mace blade
- 2 tbsp butter
- 3 tbsp all-purpose flour
- 2 tsp Dijon mustard
- generous ½ cup grated cheddar cheese
- generous ½ cup grated Gruyère cheese

1 Preheat the oven to 375°F/190°C. Heat the oil in a large, heavy-bottom pan. Add the pancetta and cook over medium heat, stirring occasionally, for 3 minutes, or until the fat starts to run. Add the onion and garlic and cook, stirring occasionally, for 5 minutes, or until softened.

2 Add the beef and cook, breaking it up with a wooden spoon, until browned all over. Stir in the celery and carrots and cook for 5 minutes. Season with salt and pepper to taste. Add the sugar, oregano, and tomatoes. Bring to a boil, reduce the heat, and let simmer for 30 minutes.

3 Meanwhile, make the cheese sauce. Pour the milk into a saucepan and add the bay leaf, peppercorns, onion, and mace. Heat gently to just below boiling point, then remove from the heat, cover, and let infuse for 10 minutes.

4 Strain the milk into a pitcher. Melt the butter in a separate saucepan. Sprinkle in the flour and cook over low heat, stirring continuously, for 1 minute. Remove from the heat and gradually stir in the warm milk. Return to the heat and bring to a boil, stirring. Cook, stirring, until thickened and smooth. Stir in the mustard, cheddar cheese, and Gruyère cheese, then season with salt and pepper to taste.

5 In a large, rectangular ovenproof dish, make alternate layers of meat sauce, lasagna noodles, and Parmesan cheese. Pour the cheese sauce over the layers, covering them completely, and sprinkle with Parmesan cheese. Bake in the preheated oven for 30 minutes, or until golden brown and bubbling. Serve immediately.

GRANDMOTHER'S TIP
This dish is quite complicated. To cheat a little, you can buy a store-bought cheese sauce to cut down on the preparation time.

Corned Beef Hash

SERVES 6

INGREDIENTS

- 2 tbsp butter
- 1 tbsp vegetable oil
- 1 lb 8 oz/675 g cooked corned beef, finely cubed
- ½ cup diced onions
- 4½ cups peeled and diced white potatoes
- ¼ tsp paprika
- ¼ tsp garlic powder
- ¼ cup diced green bell pepper, or jalapeño pepper, if a spicier version is desired
- salt and pepper
- 6 poached eggs, to serve
- 1 tbsp snipped chives, to garnish

1 Put the butter, oil, corned beef, and onions into a large, cold, nonstick or heavy-bottom skillet. Reduce the heat to medium–low and cook, stirring occasionally, while you prepare the potatoes.

2 Meanwhile, bring a large saucepan of lightly salted water to a boil, add the potatoes, and cook for 5–7 minutes, until partially cooked, but still very firm. Drain very well, then add to the skillet with the remaining ingredients.

3 Mix together thoroughly with the hot corned beef mixture, and press down slightly with a spatula to flatten. Increase the heat to medium. Every 10 minutes or so, turn the mixture over with a spatula to bring the crusty bottom up to the top. Do this several times until the mixture is well-browned, the potatoes are crispy at the edges, and the cubes of meat are caramelized.

4 Taste for salt and pepper, and adjust, if necessary. Transfer to plates and top with poached eggs. Garnish with snipped chives and serve hot.

DELICIOUS & ECONOMICAL

GRANDMOTHER'S TIP
Quick to make and delicious to eat, this is perfect served with grilled tomatoes, peas, or baked beans. If you don't like corned beef, try using leftover cooked turkey or canned tuna.

Meatloaf

SERVES 6–8

INGREDIENTS

- 3 garlic cloves, peeled
- ½ cup diced carrot
- ½ cup diced celery
- ½ cup diced yellow onion
- ½ cup diced red bell pepper
- 4 large white mushrooms, sliced
- 2 tbsp butter
- 1 tbsp olive oil, plus extra for greasing
- 1 tsp dried thyme
- 2 tsp finely chopped fresh rosemary
- 1 tsp Worcestershire sauce
- ¼ cup ketchup
- ½ tsp cayenne pepper
- 2 lb 8 oz/1.2 kg ground chuck steak, well chilled
- 2 tsp salt
- 1 tsp pepper
- 2 eggs, beaten
- 1 cup plain breadcrumbs
- Mashed Potatoes (see page 118) and peas, to serve

GLAZE

- 2 tbsp brown sugar
- 2 tbsp ketchup
- 1 tbsp Dijon mustard
- pinch of salt

1 Put the garlic, carrot, celery, onion, bell pepper, and mushrooms into a food processor. Blend on and off until the vegetables are very finely minced (several times during the processing, scrape down the sides of the bowl with a spatula so the vegetables mince evenly).

2 Add the butter and oil to a large skillet and heat over medium heat. Add the vegetable mixture and cook, stirring, for about 10 minutes, until most of the excess moisture has evaporated and the mixture is lightly caramelized.

3 Remove from the heat and stir in the thyme, rosemary, Worcestershire sauce, ketchup, and cayenne pepper. Set aside and let cool to room temperature.

4 Preheat the oven to 325°F/160°C. Put the meat into a large mixing bowl and very gently break it up with your fingertips. Pour in the cooled vegetable mixture, salt, pepper, and eggs. Gently combine with your fingertips for just 30 seconds. Add the breadcrumbs and continue mixing until combined. The less you work the meat, the better the texture of the meatloaf.

5 Lightly grease a shallow roasting pan with oil. Place the meatloaf mixture in the center of the pan. Wet your hands with cold water and form into a loaf shape about 6 inches/15 cm wide and 4 inches/10 cm high. Wet your hands again and smooth the surface. Place in the center of the preheated oven and cook for 30 minutes.

6 Meanwhile, make the glaze. Whisk all the ingredients together in a small bowl. Remove the meatloaf from the oven and spread the glaze evenly over the top with a spoon. Spread some glaze down the sides as well.

7 Return to the oven and continue baking for 35–45 minutes, or until the internal temperature reaches 155°F/70°C. Remove and let rest for at least 15 minutes before slicing and serving, accompanied by Mashed Potatoes and peas.

HEART WARMING FOOD

Spaghetti & Meatballs

SERVES 4

INGREDIENTS

- 2 tbsp olive oil, plus extra for greasing
- 1 onion, finely chopped
- 4 garlic cloves, finely chopped
- 2 tsp salt, plus a pinch of salt
- ½ tsp dried Italian herbs
- ½ loaf day-old Italian bread, crust removed
- ¼ cup milk
- 2 lb/900 g lean ground beef, well chilled
- 1 tsp pepper
- 2 extra-large eggs, beaten
- ⅓ cup chopped fresh Italian parsley
- ¾ cup freshly grated Parmesan cheese, plus extra to serve
- 6 cups marinara sauce, or other store-bought pasta sauce
- 1 cup water
- 1 lb/450 g dried spaghetti, cooked according to the package directions and drained

1 Heat the oil in a saucepan over medium–low heat and add the onion, garlic, and a pinch of salt. Sweat for 6–7 minutes, until soft and golden. Turn off heat, stir in the dried herbs, and let cool to room temperature.

2 Tear the bread into small chunks and place in a food processor (work in batches, depending on the size of the machine). Blend on and off to make fine breadcrumbs—you'll need 2 cups. Add the crumbs to a bowl and toss with the milk to moisten. Let rest for 10 minutes.

3 Put the beef, 2 teaspoons of salt, pepper, eggs, parsley, cheese, breadcrumbs, and the cooled onion mixture into a large mixing bowl, and use your hands to combine.

4 Preheat the oven to 375°F/190°C. Grease a baking sheet, then wet your hands and roll pieces of the mixture into golfball-size meatballs. Arrange the meatballs on the prepared baking sheet and bake in the preheated oven for 20 minutes. Meanwhile, add the pasta sauce and water to a large saucepan and bring to a simmer. Add the cooked meatballs to the sauce. Reduce the heat to very low, cover, and simmer gently for 45 minutes.

5 Place the cooked spaghetti in a large pasta bowl. Ladle some of the sauce over the pasta and toss to coat. Serve the spaghetti in warmed bowls, topped with the meatballs, sauce, and cheese.

GRANDMOTHER'S TIP
For the best flavor, store tomatoes in a basket in a cool place where air can circulate instead of in the refrigerator.

Fish & Fries with Peas

SERVES 4

INGREDIENTS

- vegetable oil, for deep-frying
- 6 large mealy potatoes, cut into thick strips lengthwise
- 4 thick cod fillets, about 6 oz/175 g each
- salt and pepper

BATTER

- 1¾ cups self-rising flour, plus extra for dusting
- ½ tsp salt
- 1¼ cups cold beer

PEAS

- generous 2⅓ cups frozen peas
- 2 tbsp butter
- 2 tbsp light cream

1 To make the batter, sift the flour into a bowl with a little salt and whisk in most of the beer. Check the consistency and add the remaining beer; it should be thick, like heavy cream. Let chill for 30 minutes.

2 To make the peas, bring a saucepan of lightly salted water to a boil, add the peas, and cook for 3 minutes. Drain and mash to a thick puree, add the butter and cream, then season with salt and pepper to taste. Set aside and keep warm.

3 Heat the oil to 250°F/120°C in a thermostatically controlled deep-fat fryer or large saucepan. Preheat the oven to 300°F/150°C.

4 Add the potato strips to the oil and fry for about 8–10 minutes, until softened but not colored. Remove from the oil, drain on paper towels, and place in a dish in the preheated oven.

5 Increase the temperature of the oil to 350°F/180°C.

6 Season the fish with salt and pepper to taste and dust lightly with a little flour. Dip one fillet in the batter and coat thickly.

7 Carefully place in the hot oil and repeat with the other fillets (if your fryer is small, you may need to cook 2 at a time). Cook for 8–10 minutes, turning halfway through the cooking time. Remove the fish from the oil, drain, and keep warm.

8 Reheat the oil to 350°F/180°C and cook the potatoes again for an additional 2–3 minutes, until golden brown. Drain and season with salt and pepper to taste. Serve immediately.

GRANDMOTHER'S TIP
Avoid overcrowding food in a deep-fat fryer or saucepan, since this will cause the temperature of the oil to drop. This will increase the oil absorption, resulting in a soggy batter.

Poached Salmon

SERVES 6

INGREDIENTS

- 6–8 lb/2.7–3.6 kg salmon (head on)
- 3 tbsp salt
- 3 bay leaves
- 10 peppercorns
- 1 onion, peeled and sliced
- 1 lemon, sliced
- lemon wedges, to serve

1 Wipe the salmon thoroughly inside and out with paper towels, then use the back of a cook's knife to remove any scales that might still be on the skin. Remove the fins with a pair of scissors and trim the tail. Some people prefer to remove the head but it is traditionally served with it on.

2 Place the salmon on a two-handled rack and place in a fish poacher. Fill the poacher with enough cold water to cover the salmon adequately. Sprinkle in the salt, bay leaves, and peppercorns and add the onion and lemon slices.

3 Place over two low burners and very slowly bring just to a boil.

4 Cover and simmer very gently. To serve cold, simmer for only 2 minutes, remove from the heat, and cool in the cooking liquid for about 2 hours with the lid on. To serve hot, simmer for 6–8 minutes and let the fish stand in the hot water for 15 minutes before removing. Serve with lemon wedges for squeezing over.

IMPRESS THE FAMILY

Asparagus & Tomato Quiche

SERVES 4

INGREDIENTS

- butter, for greasing
- 13 oz/375 g prepared pastry
- 1 bunch of thin asparagus spears
- 9 oz/250 g spinach leaves
- 3 extra-large eggs, beaten
- ⅔ cup heavy cream
- 1 garlic clove, crushed
- 10 small cherry tomatoes, halved
- handful of fresh basil, chopped
- ¼ cup grated Parmesan cheese
- salt and pepper

1 Preheat the oven to 375°F/190°C. Grease a 10–12-inch/25–30-cm tart pan with butter, then roll out the pastry and line the pan with it.

2 Cut off any excess, prick the bottom with a fork, cover with a piece of wax paper, and fill with dried beans, then bake it in the preheated oven for 20–30 minutes, until lightly browned. Remove from the oven and let cool slightly. Reduce the oven temperature to 350°F/180°C.

3 Meanwhile, bend the asparagus spears until they snap, and discard the woody ends. Bring a large saucepan of water to a boil, add the asparagus, and blanch for 1 minute, then remove and drain. Add the spinach to the boiling water, then remove and drain very well.

4 Mix the eggs, cream, and garlic together and season with salt and pepper to taste. Lay the blanched spinach at the bottom of the pastry shell, add the asparagus and tomatoes, cut-side up, in any arrangement you like, scatter over the basil, then pour the egg mixture on top.

5 Transfer to the oven and bake for about 35 minutes, or until the filling has set. Sprinkle over the Parmesan cheese and let cool to room temperature before serving.

GRANDMOTHER'S TIP
This is a great dish to make for summer picnics and outdoor parties. The ingredients are interchangeable with other crisp spring and summer vegetables.

Roasted Butternut Squash

SERVES 4

INGREDIENTS

- 1 butternut squash, about 1 lb/450 g
- 1 onion, chopped
- 2–3 garlic cloves, crushed
- 4 small tomatoes, chopped
- 1⅓ cups chopped cremini mushrooms
- 3 oz/85 g canned lima beans, drained, rinsed, and coarsely chopped
- 1 cup grated zucchini
- 1 tbsp chopped fresh oregano, plus extra to garnish
- 2 tbsp tomato paste
- 1¼ cups water
- 4 scallions, trimmed and chopped
- 1 tbsp Worcestershire sauce or hot pepper sauce, or to taste
- pepper

1 Preheat the oven to 375°F/190°C. Prick the squash all over with a metal skewer, then roast for 40 minutes, or until tender. Remove from the oven and let stand until cool enough to handle.

2 Cut the squash in half, scoop out and discard the seeds, then scoop out some of the flesh, making hollows in both halves. Chop the scooped-out flesh and put in a bowl. Place the two halves side by side in a large roasting pan.

3 Add the onion, garlic, tomatoes, and mushrooms to the cooked squash flesh. Add the beans, zucchini, oregano, and pepper to taste and mix well. Spoon the filling into the two halves of the squash, packing down very firmly.

4 Mix the tomato paste with the water, scallions, and Worcestershire sauce in a small bowl and pour over the squash.

5 Cover loosely with a large sheet of foil and bake for 30 minutes, or until piping hot. Serve in warmed bowls, garnished with oregano.

GRANDMOTHER'S TIP
Butternut squash is a very versatile winter fruit. It can be roasted or cooked and pureed to make a soup, or used in casseroles, breads, and even muffins.

FAIL-SAFE
SIDE DISHES
& SUNDRIES

Roasted Potatoes

SERVES 6

INGREDIENTS

- 3 lb/1.3 kg large mealy potatoes, peeled and cut into even chunks
- 3 tbsp drippings, goose fat, duck fat, or olive oil
- salt

1 Preheat the oven to 425°F/220°C.

2 Bring a large saucepan of lightly salted water to the boil, add the potatoes, and cook over medium heat, covered, for 5–7 minutes. They will still be firm. Remove from the heat.

3 Meanwhile, add the drippings to a roasting pan and place in the preheated oven.

4 Drain the potatoes well and return them to the pan. Cover with the lid and firmly shake the pan so that the surface of the potatoes is roughened to help give a much crisper texture.

5 Remove the roasting pan from the oven and carefully put the potatoes into the hot fat. Baste them to ensure they are all coated with the fat.

6 Roast at the top of the oven for 45–50 minutes, until they are browned all over and thoroughly crisp. Turn and baste again only once during the cooking process or the crunchy edges will be destroyed.

7 Carefully transfer the potatoes from the roasting pan into a warmed serving dish. Sprinkle with a little salt and serve immediately.

GUILTY PLEASURE

Sweet & Sour Red Cabbage

SERVES 6–8
INGREDIENTS

- 1 head of red cabbage
- 2 tbsp olive oil
- 2 onions, finely sliced
- 1 garlic clove, chopped
- 2 small baking apples, peeled, cored, and sliced
- 2 tbsp light brown sugar
- ½ tsp ground cinnamon
- 1 tsp crushed juniper berries
- whole nutmeg, for grating
- 2 tbsp red wine vinegar
- juice of 1 orange
- grated rind of 1 orange
- 2 tbsp cranberry jelly
- salt and pepper

1 Cut the cabbage into quarters, remove and discard the central stalk, and finely shred.

2 Heat the oil in a large saucepan and add the cabbage, onions, garlic, and apples. Sprinkle over the sugar, cinnamon, and juniper berries and grate one-quarter of the nutmeg into the pan.

3 Pour over the vinegar and orange juice and add the orange rind. Stir well and season with salt and pepper to taste.

4 Cook over medium heat, stirring occasionally, until the cabbage is just tender but still has "bite." This will take 10–15 minutes, depending on how finely the cabbage is sliced.

5 Stir in the cranberry jelly and add more salt and pepper, if necessary. Serve hot.

GRANDMOTHER'S TIP
This is the perfect winter dish and is the classic accompaniment to roasted pork. It also goes well with baked ham or sausages.

Mashed Potatoes

SERVES 4

INGREDIENTS

- 2 lb/900 g mealy potatoes
- 4 tbsp butter
- 3 tbsp hot milk
- salt and pepper

1 Peel the potatoes, placing them in cold water as you prepare the others to prevent them from turning brown.

2 Cut the potatoes into even chunks. Bring a large saucepan of lightly salted water to a boil, add the potatoes, and cook over medium heat, covered, for 20–25 minutes, until they are tender. Test with the point of a knife right to the center to avoid lumps.

3 Remove the pan from the heat and drain the potatoes. Return the potatoes to the hot pan and mash with a potato masher until smooth.

4 Add the butter and continue to mash until it is all mixed in, then add the milk.

5 Taste and season with salt and pepper as necessary. Serve immediately.

FEEL-BETTER FOOD

Asparagus with Lemon Butter Sauce

SERVES 4

INGREDIENTS

- 1 lb 12 oz/800 g asparagus spears, trimmed
- 1 tbsp olive oil
- salt and pepper

LEMON BUTTER SAUCE

- juice of ½ lemon
- 2 tbsp water
- 7 tbsp butter, cut into cubes

1 Preheat the oven to 400°F/200°C.

2 Lay the asparagus spears in a single layer on a large baking sheet. Drizzle over the oil, then season with salt and pepper to taste and roast in the preheated oven for 10 minutes, or until just tender.

3 Meanwhile, make the lemon butter sauce. Pour the lemon juice into a saucepan and add the water. Heat for a minute or so, then slowly add the butter, cube by cube, stirring continuously, until it has all been incorporated. Season with pepper to taste and serve immediately with the asparagus.

GRANDMOTHER'S TIP
Fresh asparagus will keep for 3 or 4 days in the refrigerator. Do not wash before storing, but just before using.

QUICK & SIMPLE FIX

Potato & Cabbage Pancake

SERVES 2–3

INGREDIENTS

- 1 lb/45 g green cabbage
- 4 tbsp olive oil
- 1 onion, thinly sliced
- salt and pepper

MASHED POTATOES

- 2 large mealy potatoes, peeled and cut into chunks
- 4 tbsp butter
- 3 tbsp hot milk

1 To make the mashed potatoes, bring a large saucepan of lightly salted water to a boil, add the potatoes, and cook for 15–20 minutes. Drain well and mash with a potato masher until smooth. Season with salt and pepper, add the butter and milk, and stir well.

2 Cut the cabbage into quarters, remove the center stalk, and finely shred.

3 Add half of the oil to a large skillet, then add the onion and fry until softened. Add the cabbage and stir-fry for 2–3 minutes, until softened. Season with salt and pepper, add the mashed potatoes, and mix well together.

4 Press the mixture firmly into the skillet and let cook over high heat for 4–5 minutes, until the bottom is crisp. Place a plate over the skillet and invert the skillet so that the pancake falls onto the plate. Add the remaining oil to the skillet, reheat, and slip the pancake back into the skillet, uncooked-side down.

5 Continue to cook for an additional 5 minutes, until the bottom is crisp. Turn out onto a warmed plate, cut into wedges, and serve immediately.

GRANDMOTHER'S TIP
This is a great way to use up leftovers. Chopped Brussels sprouts can be substituted for the cabbage.

Hush Puppies

MAKES 30–35 HUSH PUPPIES
INGREDIENTS

- 2 cups yellow cornmeal
- ½ cup all-purpose flour, sifted
- 1 small onion, finely chopped
- 1 tbsp superfine sugar
- 2 tsp baking powder
- pinch of salt
- ¾ cup milk
- 1 egg, beaten
- corn oil, for deep-frying

1 Stir the cornmeal, flour, onion, sugar, baking powder, and salt together in a bowl and make a well in the center.

2 Beat the milk and egg together in a pitcher, then pour into the dry ingredients and stir until a thick batter forms.

3 Heat at least 2 inches/ 5 cm of oil in a deep skillet or saucepan over high heat, until the temperature reaches 350°F/180°C, or until a cube of bread browns in 30 seconds.

4 Drop in as many teaspoonfuls of the batter as will fit without overcrowding the skillet and cook, stirring continuously, until the hush puppies puff up and turn golden.

5 Remove from the oil with a slotted spoon and drain on paper towels. Reheat the oil, if necessary, and cook the remaining batter. Serve hot.

GRANDMOTHER'S TIP
Variations of the hush puppies can be made by adding cheese or vegetables to the batter before frying.

Brussels Sprouts with Chestnuts

SERVES 4

INGREDIENTS

- 12 oz/350 g Brussels
  sprouts, trimmed
- 3 tbsp butter
- 3½ oz/100 g canned
  whole chestnuts
- pinch of grated nutmeg
- salt and pepper
- ½ cup slivered almonds,
  to garnish

1 Bring a large saucepan of lightly salted water to a boil. Add the Brussels sprouts and cook for 5 minutes. Drain thoroughly.

2 Melt the butter in a large saucepan over medium heat. Add the Brussels sprouts and cook, stirring, for 3 minutes, then add the chestnuts and nutmeg.

3 Season with salt and pepper to taste and stir well. Cook for an additional 2 minutes, stirring, then remove from the heat.

4 Transfer to a warmed serving dish, then scatter over the almonds and serve.

IDEAL
WINTER WARMER

GRANDMOTHER'S TIP
If you can buy Brussels sprouts still attached to their long central stalk, so much the better. They'll keep fresh for longer that way.

Scalloped Potatoes

SERVES 8

INGREDIENTS

- 2 tbsp butter
- 1 tbsp all-purpose flour
- 1 cup cream
- 2 cups milk
- pinch of nutmeg
- pinch of white pepper
- 4 sprigs fresh thyme
- 2 garlic cloves, finely chopped
- 1 tsp salt
- 4 lb 8 oz/2 kg russet potatoes, thinly sliced
- 1 cup grated Gruyère cheese or cheddar cheese
- salt and pepper

1 Preheat the oven to 375°F/190°C. Use half of the butter to grease a 15 x 10-inch/38 x 25-cm baking dish.

2 Melt the remaining butter in a saucepan over medium heat. Whisk in the flour, and cook, stirring continuously, for 2 minutes. Whisk in the cream and milk, and bring to a simmer. Add the nutmeg, white pepper, thyme, garlic, and salt. Reduce the heat to low and simmer for 5 minutes. Remove the thyme sprigs and reserve.

3 Layer half of the potatoes in the baking dish. Season generously with salt and pepper. Top with half of the sauce, then scatter over half of the cheese. Repeat with the remaining potatoes, sauce, and cheese.

4 Bake in the preheated oven for about 1 hour, or until the top is browned and the potatoes are tender. Let rest for 15 minutes before serving.

GRANDMOTHER'S TIP
These creamy, garlicky potatoes make the perfect side dish for any roasted meat.

Roasted Root Vegetables

SERVES 4–6

INGREDIENTS

- 3 parsnips, cut into
  2-inch/5-cm chunks
- 4 baby turnips, quartered
- 3 carrots, cut into
  2-inch/5-cm chunks
- 1 lb/450 g butternut
  squash, peeled and cut into
  2-inch/5-cm chunks
- 1 lb/450 g sweet potatoes,
  peeled and cut into
  2-inch/5-cm chunks
- 2 garlic cloves,
  finely chopped
- 2 tbsp chopped
  fresh rosemary
- 2 tbsp chopped fresh thyme
- 2 tsp chopped fresh sage
- 3 tbsp olive oil
- salt and pepper
- 2 tbsp chopped fresh mixed
  herbs, such as flat-leaf
  parsley, thyme, and mint,
  to garnish

1 Preheat the oven to 425°F/220°C.

2 Arrange all the vegetables in a single layer in a large roasting pan. Sprinkle over the garlic and the herbs. Pour the oil and season well with salt and pepper.

3 Toss all the ingredients together until they are well mixed and coated with the oil (you can let them marinate at this stage so that the flavors can be absorbed).

4 Roast the vegetables at the top of the preheated oven for 50–60 minutes, until they are cooked and nicely browned. Turn the vegetables over halfway through the cooking time.

5 Serve with a good handful of fresh herbs sprinkled on top and a final seasoning of salt and pepper to taste.

DELICIOUS & ECONOMICAL

Zucchini Fritters

MAKES 20–30 FRITTERS

INGREDIENTS

- ¾ cup self-rising flour
- 2 eggs, beaten
- 4 tbsp milk
- 1 large zucchini
- 2 tbsp fresh thyme, plus extra to garnish
- 1 tbsp oil
- salt and pepper

1 Sift the flour into a large bowl and make a well in the center. Add the eggs to the well and, using a wooden spoon, gradually draw in the flour.

2 Slowly add the milk to the mixture, stirring continuously to form a thick batter.

3 Grate the zucchini over a few paper towels placed in a bowl to absorb some of the juices.

4 Add the zucchini, thyme, and salt and pepper to taste to the batter and mix thoroughly, for about a minute.

5 Heat the oil in a large, heavy-bottom skillet. Taking 1 tablespoon of the batter for a medium fritter or ½ tablespoon of batter for a smaller fritter, spoon the mixture into the hot oil and cook, in batches, for 3–4 minutes on each side.

6 Remove the fritters with a slotted spoon and drain thoroughly on absorbent paper towels. Keep each batch of fritters warm in the oven while making the rest. Transfer to serving plates and serve hot, garnished with thyme.

Coleslaw

SERVES 10–12

INGREDIENTS

- ⅔ cup mayonnaise
- ⅔ cup plain yogurt
- dash of Tabasco sauce
- 1 head of white cabbage
- 4 carrots
- 1 green bell pepper
- salt and pepper

1 To make the dressing, mix the mayonnaise, yogurt, Tabasco sauce, and salt and pepper to taste together in a small bowl. Chill in the refrigerator until required.

2 Cut the cabbage in half and then into quarters. Remove and discard the tough center stem and finely shred the leaves. Wash the leaves under cold running water and dry thoroughly on paper towels. Peel the carrots and roughly grate or shred in a food processor or on a mandolin. Seed the bell pepper, then cut the flesh into thin strips.

3 Mix the vegetables together in a large serving bowl and toss to mix. Pour over the dressing and toss until the vegetables are well coated. Let chill until ready to serve.

GRANDMOTHER'S TIP
You can add in plenty of other ingredients to add taste, color, and texture, such as smoked almonds, capers, apples, toasted pecans, sunflower seeds, and pumpkin seeds.

Red Wine Sauce

MAKES ABOUT 1 CUP

INGREDIENTS

- ⅔ cup Gravy (see page 137)
- 4 tbsp red wine,
  such as a Burgundy
- 1 tbsp red currant jelly

1 Blend the gravy with the wine and pour into a small heavy-bottom pan. Add the red currant jelly and warm over gentle heat, stirring, until blended.

2 Bring to a boil, then reduce the heat and simmer for 2 minutes. Serve hot.

GRANDMOTHER'S TIP
For a richer sauce, ideal as an accompaniment to game dishes, replace half of the red wine with Marsala, sherry, or port.

Gravy

MAKES ABOUT 5 CUPS
INGREDIENTS

• 2 lb/900 g meat bones,
  raw or cooked
• 1 large onion, chopped
• 1 large carrot, chopped
• 2 celery stalks, chopped
• 1 bouquet garni
• 8 cups water

1 Preheat the oven to 400°F/200°C. Put the bones in a roasting pan and roast in the preheated oven for 20 minutes, or until browned. Remove from the oven and let cool.

2 Chop the bones into small pieces and put in a large saucepan with all the remaining ingredients. Bring to a boil, then reduce the heat, cover, and simmer for 2 hours.

3 Strain and let stand until cold, then remove all traces of fat. Store, covered, in the refrigerator for up to 4 days. Boil vigorously for 5 minutes before using. The gravy can be frozen in ice-cube trays for up to 1 month.

Mint & Spinach Relish

SERVES 4–6

INGREDIENTS

- 2 cups tender fresh
  spinach leaves
- 3 tbsp fresh mint leaves
- 2 tbsp chopped fresh
  cilantro leaves
- 1 small red onion,
  coarsely chopped
- 1 small garlic clove, chopped
- 1 fresh green chile, chopped
- 2½ tsp sugar
- 1 tbsp tamarind juice or juice
  of ½ lemon

1 Place all the ingredients in a food processor and process until smooth, adding only as much water as necessary to enable the blades to move.

2 Transfer to a serving bowl, cover, and let chill in the refrigerator for at least 30 minutes before serving.

GRANDMOTHER'S TIP
For an even cooler relish to serve with very spicy dishes, omit the spinach, double the quantity of cilantro, and seed the chile.

Bread Sauce

SERVES 6–9

INGREDIENTS

- 1 onion
- 12 cloves
- 1 bay leaf
- 6 black peppercorns
- 2½ cups milk
- 2 cups fresh
  white breadcrumbs
- 2 tbsp butter
- whole nutmeg, for grating
- 2 tbsp heavy cream (optional)
- salt and pepper

1 Make small holes in the onion using the point of a sharp knife or a skewer, and stick the cloves in them.

2 Put the onion, bay leaf, and peppercorns in a saucepan and pour in the milk. Bring to a boil, then remove from the heat, cover, and set aside to infuse for 1 hour.

3 Discard the onion and bay leaf and strain the milk to remove the peppercorns. Return the milk to the cleaned pan and add the breadcrumbs.

4 Cook the sauce over very low heat for 4–5 minutes, until the breadcrumbs have swollen and the sauce is thick.

5 Beat in the butter and season well with salt and pepper and a good grating of nutmeg. Stir in the cream just before serving, if using.

Corn Relish

MAKES ABOUT 2½ CUPS
INGREDIENTS

- 5 corn cobs,
  about 2 lb/900 g, husked
- 1 red bell pepper, seeded
  and finely diced
- 2 celery stalks,
  very finely chopped
- 1 red onion, finely chopped
- ½ cup plus 2 tbsp sugar
- 1 tbsp salt
- 2 tbsp dry mustard
- ½ tsp celery seeds
- small pinch of
  turmeric (optional)
- 1 cup apple cider vinegar
- ½ cup water

1 Bring a large saucepan of lightly salted water to a boil and fill a bowl with iced water. Add the corn to the boiling water, return to a boil, and boil for 2 minutes, or until the kernels are tender-crisp. Using tongs, immediately plunge the cobs into the cold water to halt cooking. Remove the cobs from the water and cut off the kernels, then set aside.

2 Add the bell pepper, celery, and onion to the corn cooking water, return to a boil, and boil for 2 minutes, or until tender-crisp. Drain well and return to the pan with the corn kernels.

3 Put the sugar, salt, mustard, celery seeds, and turmeric, if using, into a bowl and mix together, then stir in the vinegar and water. Add to the pan, bring the liquid to a boil, then reduce the heat and simmer for 15 minutes, stirring occasionally.

4 Ladle the relish into hot, sterilized preserving jars, filling them to within ½ inch/1 cm of the top of each jar. Wipe the rims and secure the lids. Let the relish cool completely, then refrigerate for up to 2 months.

PRACTICE MAKES PERFECT

White Chocolate Fudge Sauce

SERVES 4

INGREDIENTS

- ⅔ cup heavy cream
- 4 tbsp unsalted butter,
  cut into small pieces
- 3 tbsp superfine sugar
- 6 oz/175 g white chocolate,
  broken into pieces
- 2 tbsp brandy

1 Pour the cream into the top of a double boiler or a heatproof bowl set over a saucepan of gently simmering water. Add the butter and sugar and stir until smooth. Remove from the heat.

2 Stir in the chocolate, a few pieces at a time, waiting until each batch has melted before adding the next. Add the brandy and stir the sauce until smooth. Let cool to room temperature before serving.

GRANDMOTHER'S TIP
You can give this sauce a citrussy zing by replacing the brandy with the same quantity of an orange liqueur, such as Cointreau or Grand Marnier.

Chocolate Brandy Sauce

SERVES 4

INGREDIENTS

- 9 oz/250 g semisweet chocolate (must contain at least 50 percent cocoa solids)
- ½ cup heavy cream
- 2 tbsp brandy

1 Break or chop the chocolate into small pieces and place in the top of a double boiler or in a heatproof bowl set over a pan of simmering water.

2 Pour in the cream and stir until melted and smooth. Stir in the brandy, pour into a pitcher, and serve.

IMPRESS THE FAMILY

Homemade Custard

INGREDIENTS

- 1¼ cups milk
- 2 extra-large eggs
- 2 tsp superfine sugar
- 1 vanilla bean, split, or 1 tsp vanilla extract

1 Put 2 tablespoons of the milk, the eggs, and sugar into a heatproof bowl that will fit over a saucepan of simmering water without the bottom of the bowl touching the water, then set aside.

2 Put the remaining milk into a small, heavy-bottom saucepan over medium–high heat and heat just until small bubbles appear around the edge. Scrape half of the vanilla seeds into the milk and add the bean. Remove the pan from the heat, cover, and let infuse for 30 minutes.

3 Bring a kettle of water to a boil. Meanwhile, using an electric mixer, beat the milk, eggs, and sugar until pale and thick. Slowly beat in the warm milk.

4 Bring a thin layer of water in a saucepan to a boil, reduce the heat to low, and fit the bowl containing the milk mixture snugly on top. Cook, stirring continuously, for 10–15 minutes, until the sauce becomes thick enough to hold the impression of your finger if you rub it along the back of the spoon. It is important that the bottom of the bowl never touches the water and that the sauce doesn't boil. If the sauce looks as if it is about to boil, remove the bowl from the pan and continue stirring.

5 Strain the hot custard into a separate bowl. If you have not used a vanilla bean and seeds, stir in the vanilla extract. The custard can be used immediately, or let cool completely, then covered and chilled for up to 1 day. It will thicken as it cools.

GRANDMOTHER'S TIP
The vanilla bean can be rinsed, thoroughly dried, and saved to use again.

BEST-EVER
BAKING DAY

Pineapple Upside-Down Cake

SERVES 10
INGREDIENTS

- 4 eggs, beaten
- 1 cup superfine sugar
- 1 tsp vanilla extract
- 1¾ cups all-purpose flour
- 2 tsp baking powder
- generous ½ cup unsalted butter, melted, plus extra for greasing

TOPPING

- 3 tbsp unsalted butter
- 4 tbsp light corn syrup
- 15 oz/425 g canned pineapple rings, drained
- 4–6 candied cherries, halved

1 Preheat the oven to 325°F/160°C. Grease a deep 9-inch/23-cm round cake pan with a solid bottom and line the bottom with parchment paper.

2 To make the topping, place the butter and corn syrup in a heavy-bottom saucepan and heat gently until melted. Bring to a boil and boil for 2–3 minutes, stirring, until slightly thickened and taffylike.

3 Pour the syrup into the bottom of the prepared pan. Arrange the pineapple rings and cherries in a single layer over the syrup.

4 Place the eggs, sugar, and vanilla extract in a large heatproof bowl set over a saucepan of gently simmering water and beat with an electric mixer for 10–15 minutes, until thick enough to leave a trail when the beaters are lifted. Sift in the flour and baking powder and fold in lightly and evenly with a metal spoon.

5 Fold the butter into the mixture with a metal spoon until evenly mixed. Spoon into the prepared pan and bake in the preheated oven for 1–1¼ hours, or until well risen, firm, and golden brown.

6 Let cool in the pan for 10 minutes, then carefully turn out onto a serving plate. Serve warm or cold.

GRANDMOTHER'S TIP
If your cake sinks in the center, cut it out to make a ring cake, spread with whipped cream, and fill the center with fresh berries.

Raspberry Sponge Cake

SERVES 8–10

INGREDIENTS

- ¾ cup unsalted butter, at room temperature, plus extra for greasing
- ¾ cup superfine sugar
- 3 eggs, beaten
- scant 1½ cups self-rising flour
- pinch of salt
- 3 tbsp raspberry jelly
- confectioners' sugar, for dusting

1 Preheat the oven to 350°F/180°C.

2 Grease two 8-inch/20-cm round cake pans and line with parchment paper.

3 Cream the butter and sugar together in a mixing bowl using a wooden spoon or a handheld mixer, until the mixture is pale in color and light and fluffy.

4 Add the eggs, one at a time, beating well after each addition.

5 Sift the flour and salt together into a separate bowl and carefully add to the mixture, folding it in with a metal spoon or a spatula. Divide the mixture between the prepared pans, smoothing the surface.

6 Place the pans in the center of the preheated oven and bake for 25–30 minutes, until the cakes are well risen, golden brown, and beginning to shrink from the sides of the pans.

7 Remove from the oven and let stand for 1 minute.

8 Loosen the cakes from around the edge of the pans using a palette knife. Turn out onto a clean dish towel, remove the paper, and invert the cakes onto a wire rack (this prevents the wire rack from marking the top of the cakes).

9 When completely cool, sandwich the cakes together with the jelly and sprinkle with confectioners' sugar. The cake is delicious when freshly baked, but any remaining cake can be stored in an airtight container for up to 1 week.

FEEL-BETTER FOOD

Crumb Cake

INGREDIENTS

- 2 cups fresh blueberries
- 3 cups self-rising flour, plus extra for dusting
- 1¼ tsp salt
- ½ tsp apple pie spice
- 1¼ cups butter, at room temperature, plus extra for greasing
- 1¾ cups superfine sugar
- ½ tsp vanilla extract
- ½ tsp almond extract
- 2 extra-large eggs
- 1¼– 1½ cups sour cream

ALMOND STREUSEL TOPPING

- ½ cup butter, diced
- 1 cup all-purpose flour
- 2 tbsp light brown sugar
- 1 tbsp granulated sugar
- generous ¼ cup chopped blanched almonds

1 To make the almond streusel topping, put the butter and flour into a large bowl and rub together until coarse crumbs form. Stir in both types of sugar and the almonds, then let chill in the refrigerator until required.

2 Preheat the oven to 350°F/180°C. Butter a 13 x 9-inch/33 x 23-cm rectangular cake pan and dust with flour. Dust the blueberries with 1 tablespoon of the measured flour and set aside. Sift the remaining flour into a bowl with the salt and apple pie spice and set aside.

3 Place the butter in a large bowl and, using an electric mixer, beat until soft and creamy. Add the sugar, vanilla extract, and almond extract and continue beating until the mixture is

light and fluffy. Add the eggs, one at a time, beating well after each addition, then beat in 1¼ cups of the sour cream. Beat in the flour until the mixture is soft and falls easily from a spoon. Add the remaining sour cream, 1 tablespoon at a time, if necessary.

4 Add the blueberries and any loose flour to the batter and quickly fold in. Pour the batter into the prepared pan and smooth the surface. Pinch the topping into large crumbs and scatter evenly over the batter.

5 Bake the cake in the preheated oven for 45–55 minutes, until it comes away from the side of the pan and a toothpick inserted in the center comes out clean. Transfer the pan to a wire rack and let the cake cool completely. Cut into 12 slices and serve straight from the pan.

GRANDMOTHER'S TIP
When a recipe says "dot with butter," shave off curls from a cold stick with a vegetable peeler.

Angel Food Cake

SERVES 10

INGREDIENTS

- sunflower oil, for greasing
- 8 extra-large egg whites
- 1 tsp cream of tartar
- 1 tsp almond extract
- 1¼ cups superfine sugar
- 1 cup all-purpose flour, plus extra for dusting

TO SERVE

- 2¼ cups berries, such as strawberries and raspberries
- 1 tbsp lemon juice
- 2 tbsp confectioners' sugar

1 Preheat the oven to 325°F/160°C. Brush the inside of a 7½-cup angel cake pan with oil and dust lightly with flour.

2 In a large grease-free bowl, whisk the egg whites until they hold soft peaks. Add the cream of tartar and whisk again until the whites are stiff but not dry.

3 Whisk in the almond extract, then add the sugar a tablespoon at a time, whisking hard between each addition. Sift in the flour and fold in lightly and evenly using a large metal spoon.

4 Spoon the batter into the prepared cake pan and tap on the counter to remove any large air bubbles. Bake in the preheated oven for 40–45 minutes, or until golden brown and firm to the touch.

5 Run the tip of a small knife around the edge of the cake to loosen it from the pan. Let cool in the pan for 10 minutes, then turn out onto a wire rack to finish cooling.

6 To serve, place the berries, lemon juice, and confectioners' sugar in a saucepan and heat gently until the sugar has dissolved. Serve with the cake.

GRANDMOTHER'S TIP
The delicious Angel Food Cake takes its name from its light and airy white sponge.

Devil's Food Cake

SERVES 8–10

INGREDIENTS

- 5 oz/140 g semisweet chocolate
- scant ½ cup milk
- 2 tbsp unsweetened cocoa
- ⅔ cup butter, plus extra for greasing
- ⅔ cup light brown sugar
- 3 eggs, separated
- 4 tbsp sour cream
- 1¾ cups all-purpose flour
- 1 tsp baking soda

FROSTING

- 5 oz/140 g semisweet chocolate
- ⅓ cup unsweetened cocoa
- 4 tbsp sour cream
- 1 tbsp light corn syrup
- 3 tbsp butter
- 4 tbsp water
- 1¾ cups confectioners' sugar

1 Preheat the oven to 325°F/160°C. Grease and line the bottoms of two 8-inch/20-cm round cake pans.

2 Break up the chocolate and place with the milk and cocoa in a heatproof bowl set over over a saucepan of gently simmering water, stirring until melted and smooth. Remove from the heat.

3 In a large bowl, beat together the butter and sugar until pale and fluffy. Beat in the egg yolks, then the sour cream and melted chocolate mixture.

4 Sift in the flour and baking soda, then fold in evenly. In a separate bowl, whip the egg whites until stiff enough to hold firm peaks. Fold into the mixture lightly and evenly.

5 Divide the batter between the prepared cake pans, smooth the surfaces, and bake in the preheated oven for 35–40 minutes, or until risen and firm to the touch. Let cool in the pans for 10 minutes, then turn out onto a wire rack.

6 To make the frosting, place the chocolate, cocoa, sour cream, corn syrup, butter, and water in a saucepan and heat gently, without boiling, until melted. Remove from the heat and add the sugar, stirring until smooth. Let cool, stirring occasionally, until the mixture begins to thicken and hold its shape.

7 Split each cake in half horizontally with a sharp knife to make four layers. Sandwich the cakes together with about one-third of the frosting. Spread the remainder over the top and sides of the cakes swirling with a spatula.

GRANDMOTHER'S TIP
Use a metal, ceramic, or glass bowl when whisking egg whites. Plastic bowls scratch easily, so may not be grease-free, and will prevent the whites from foaming.

Lemon Pound Cake

SERVES 8

INGREDIENTS

- butter, for greasing
- 1¾ cups all-purpose flour
- 2 tsp baking powder
- 1 cup superfine sugar
- 4 eggs
- ⅔ cup sour cream
- grated rind of 1 large lemon
- 4 tbsp lemon juice
- ⅔ cup sunflower oil

SYRUP

- 4 tbsp confectioners' sugar
- 3 tbsp lemon juice

1 Preheat the oven to 350°F/180°C. Lightly grease an 8-inch/20-cm loose-bottom round cake pan and line the bottom with parchment paper.

2 Sift the flour and baking powder together into a mixing bowl and stir in the sugar.

3 In a separate bowl, whisk the eggs, sour cream, lemon rind, lemon juice, and oil together.

4 Pour the egg mixture into the dry ingredients and mix well until evenly combined.

5 Pour the mixture into the prepared pan and bake in the preheated oven for 45–60 minutes, or until risen and golden brown.

6 Meanwhile, to make the syrup, mix the sugar and lemon juice together in a small pan. Stir over low heat until just beginning to bubble and turn syrupy.

7 As soon as the cake comes out of the oven, prick the surface with a fine skewer, then brush the syrup over the top. Let the cake cool completely in the pan before turning out and serving.

GUILTY PLEASURE

Apple Cake

SERVES 8

INGREDIENTS

- 1 lb/450 g baking apples
- 1¼ cups self-rising flour
- 1 tsp ground cinnamon
- pinch of salt
- ½ cup butter, plus extra for greasing
- generous ½ cup superfine sugar
- 2 eggs
- 1–2 tbsp milk
- confectioners' sugar, for dusting

STREUSEL TOPPING

- generous ¾ cup self-rising flour
- 6 tbsp butter
- scant ½ cup superfine sugar

1 Preheat the oven to 350°F/180°C, then grease a 9-inch/23-cm springform cake pan. To make the streusel topping, sift the flour into a bowl and rub in the butter until the mixture resembles coarse crumbs. Stir in the sugar and set aside.

2 Peel, core, and thinly slice the apples. To make the cake, sift the flour into a bowl with the cinnamon and salt. Place the butter and sugar in a separate bowl and beat together until light and fluffy. Gradually beat in the eggs, adding a little of the flour mixture with the last addition of egg. Gently fold in half of the remaining flour mixture, then fold in the rest with the milk.

3 Spoon the batter into the prepared pan and smooth the top. Cover with the sliced apples and sprinkle the streusel topping evenly over the top.

4 Bake in the preheated oven for 1 hour, or until browned and firm to the touch. Let cool in the pan before opening the sides. Dust the cake with confectioners' sugar before serving.

FEEL-BETTER FOOD

Chocolate Caramel Shortbread

MAKES 12 SLICES

INGREDIENTS

- ½ cup butter, plus extra for greasing
- generous 1 cup all-purpose flour
- generous ¼ cup superfine sugar
- 7 oz/200 g semisweet chocolate, broken into pieces

FILLING

- ¾ cup butter
- generous ½ cup superfine sugar
- 3 tbsp light corn syrup
- 14 oz/400 g canned sweetened condensed milk

1 Preheat the oven to 350°F/180°C. Grease a shallow 9-inch/23-cm square, cake pan and line the bottom with parchment paper.

2 Place the butter, flour, and sugar in a food processor and process until it starts to bind together. Press into the prepared pan and level the top. Bake in the preheated oven for 20–25 minutes, or until golden.

3 Meanwhile, make the filling. Place the butter, sugar, corn syrup, and condensed milk in a heavy-bottom saucepan. Heat gently until the sugar has dissolved.

4 Bring to a boil, then reduce the heat and let simmer for 6–8 minutes, stirring, until very thick. Pour over the shortbread and let chill in the refrigerator for 2 hours, or until firm.

5 Place the chocolate in a heatproof bowl set over a saucepan of gently simmering water and stir until melted. Let cool slightly, then spread over the caramel. Let chill in the refrigerator for 2 hours, or until set. Cut the shortbread into 12 pieces and serve.

GRANDMOTHER'S TIP
This delicious shortbread is thought to originate in Scotland, where it is known as Millionaires' Shortbread.

Classic Oatmeal Cookies

MAKES 30 COOKIES

INGREDIENTS

- ¾ cup butter or margarine, plus extra for greasing
- scant 1⅓ cups raw brown sugar
- 1 egg
- 4 tbsp water
- 1 tsp vanilla extract
- 4⅓ cups rolled oats
- 1 cup all-purpose flour
- 1 tsp salt
- ½ tsp baking soda

1 Preheat the oven to 350°F/180°C and grease a large cookie sheet.

2 Cream the butter and sugar together in a large mixing bowl. Beat in the egg, water, and vanilla extract until the mixture is smooth. In a separate bowl, mix the oats, flour, salt, and baking soda together.

3 Gradually stir the oat mixture into the butter mixture until thoroughly combined.

4 Put tablespoonfuls of the mixture onto the prepared cookie sheet, making sure they are well spaced. Transfer to the preheated oven and bake for 15 minutes, or until the cookies are golden brown.

5 Using a palette knife, carefully transfer the cookies to wire racks to cool completely.

Mega Chip Cookies

MAKES 12 LARGE COOKIES

INGREDIENTS

- 1 cup butter, softened
- scant ¾ cup superfine sugar
- 1 egg yolk, lightly beaten
- 2 tsp vanilla extract
- 2 cups all-purpose flour
- ½ cup unsweetened cocoa
- pinch of salt
- ½ cup milk chocolate chips
- ½ cup white chocolate chips
- 4 oz/115 g bittersweet
  chocolate, coarsely chopped

1 Preheat the oven to 375°F/190°C. Line 2–3 cookie sheets with baking parchment.

2 Put the butter and sugar into a bowl and mix well with a wooden spoon, then beat in the egg yolk and vanilla extract. Sift the flour, cocoa, and salt together into the mixture, add both kinds of chocolate chips, and stir until thoroughly combined.

3 Make 12 balls of the mixture, put them on the prepared cookie sheets, spaced well apart, and flatten slightly. Press the pieces of bittersweet chocolate into the cookies.

4 Bake for 12–15 minutes. Let cool on the cookie sheets for 5–10 minutes, then, using a metal spatula, carefully transfer to wire racks to cool completely.

Chocolate Brownies

MAKES 16 BROWNIES

INGREDIENTS

- peanut oil, for greasing
- 8 squares good-quality semisweet chocolate, at least 60 percent cocoa solids
- ¾ cup butter
- 3 extra-large eggs
- ½ cup superfine sugar
- scant 1¼ cups self-rising flour
- 1 cup walnuts or blanched hazelnuts, chopped
- scant ⅓ cup milk chocolate chips

1 Preheat the oven to 350°F/180°C. Lightly grease a nonstick baking sheet, about 10 inches/25 cm square.

2 Break the chocolate into a heatproof bowl that will fit snugly over a small saucepan, so that when you put ¾ inch/2 cm water in the saucepan, the bottom of the bowl doesn't touch the water.

3 Add the butter to the chocolate, then set the bowl over the saucepan and heat the water to a slow simmer. Let the chocolate stand undisturbed to melt very slowly—this will take about 10 minutes. Remove the bowl from the pan and stir well to combine the chocolate and butter.

4 Meanwhile, beat the eggs and sugar together in a bowl until pale cream in color. Stir in the melted chocolate mixture and then the flour, nuts, and chocolate chips. Mix everything together well.

5 Turn the mixture into the prepared baking pan and bake in the preheated oven for 30 minutes, or until the top is set—if the center is still slightly sticky, that will be all the better. Let cool in the pan, then lift out and cut into squares.

CHILDREN'S FAVORITE

Butterfly Cupcakes

MAKES 12 CUPCAKES

INGREDIENTS

- generous ¾ cup self-rising flour
- ½ tsp baking powder
- ½ cup butter, softened
- heaping ½ cup superfine sugar
- 2 eggs, beaten
- finely grated rind of ½ lemon
- 2–4 tbsp milk
- confectioners' sugar, for dusting

FILLING
- 4 tbsp butter
- generous 1 cup confectioners' sugar
- 1 tbsp lemon juice

1 Preheat the oven to 375°F/190°C. Place 12 paper liners in a muffin pan. Sift the flour and baking powder into a bowl. Add the butter, sugar, eggs, lemon rind, and enough milk to give a medium–soft consistency.

2 Beat thoroughly until smooth. Divide the batter among the paper liners and bake in the preheated oven for 15–20 minutes, or until well risen and golden. Transfer to wire racks to cool.

3 To make the filling, place the butter in a bowl, then sift in the sugar and add the lemon juice. Beat well until smooth and creamy. When the cakes are completely cooled, use a sharp-pointed vegetable knife to cut a circle from the top of each cake, then cut each circle in half.

4 Spoon a little of the buttercream into the center of each cake and press the two semicircular pieces into it to resemble wings. Dust the cakes with confectioners' sugar before serving.

GRANDMOTHER'S TIP
Cupcakes are always a favorite with children. You can use multicolored or patterned paper liners to make these look even cuter.

Bran Muffins with Raisins

MAKES 12 MUFFINS

INGREDIENTS

- 1 cup all-purpose flour
- 1 tbsp baking powder
- 2¼ cups wheat bran
- generous ½ cup superfine sugar
- 1 cup raisins
- 2 extra-large eggs
- 1 cup skim milk
- 6 tbsp sunflower oil
- 1 tsp vanilla extract

1 Preheat the oven to 400°F/200°C. Grease a 12-cup muffin pan or line with 12 muffin paper liners. Sift the flour and baking powder together into a large bowl. Stir in the bran, sugar, and raisins.

2 Lightly beat the eggs in a large pitcher or bowl, then beat in the milk, oil, and vanilla extract. Make a well in the center of the dry ingredients and pour in the beaten liquid ingredients. Stir gently until just combined; do not overmix.

3 Spoon the batter into the prepared muffin pan. Bake in the preheated oven for about 20 minutes, until well risen, golden brown, and firm to the touch.

4 Let the muffins cool in the pan for 5 minutes, then serve warm or transfer to a wire rack and let cool completely.

Cinnamon Swirls

MAKES 12 SWIRLS
INGREDIENTS

- 1⅔ cups white bread flour
- ½ tsp salt
- 3¼ oz/10 g active dry yeast
- 2 tbsp butter, cut into small pieces, plus extra for greasing
- 1 egg, lightly beaten
- ½ cup lukewarm milk
- 2 tbsp maple syrup, for glazing

FILLING
- 4 tbsp butter, softened
- 2 tsp ground cinnamon
- ¼ cup light brown sugar
- ⅓ cup currants

1 Grease a baking sheet with a little butter.

2 Sift the flour and salt into a mixing bowl. Stir in the yeast. Rub in the butter with your fingertips until the mixture resembles breadcrumbs. Add the egg and milk and mix to form a dough.

3 Form the dough into a ball, place in a greased bowl, cover, and let stand in a warm place for about 40 minutes, or until doubled in size.

4 Punch down the dough lightly for 1 minute, then roll out to a rectangle measuring 12 x 9 inches/ 30 x 23 cm.

5 To make the filling, cream together the butter, cinnamon, and brown sugar until light and fluffy. Spread the filling evenly over the dough rectangle, leaving a 1-inch/ 2.5-cm border all around. Sprinkle the currants evenly over the top.

6 Roll up the dough from one of the long edges, and press down to seal. Cut the roll into 12 slices. Place them, cut-side down, on the baking sheet, cover, and let stand for 30 minutes.

7 Meanwhile, preheat the oven to 375°F/ 190°C. Bake the swirls in the preheated oven for 20–30 minutes, or until well risen. Brush with the maple syrup and let cool slightly before serving.

Strawberry Shortcakes

SERVES 6

INGREDIENTS

- 2 cups self-rising flour, plus extra for dusting
- ½ tsp baking powder
- ½ cup superfine sugar
- 6 tbsp unsalted butter, plus extra for greasing
- 1 egg, beaten
- 2–3 tbsp milk, plus extra for brushing

FILLING

- 1 tsp vanilla extract
- generous 1 cup mascarpone cheese
- 3 tbsp confectioners' sugar, plus extra for dusting
- 3½ cups strawberries

1 Preheat the oven to 350°F/180°C and lightly grease a large baking sheet.

2 Sift the flour, baking powder, and sugar into a bowl. Rub in the butter with your fingertips until the mixture resembles breadcrumbs. Beat the egg with 2 tablespoons of the milk and stir into the dry ingredients with a fork to form a soft, but not sticky, dough, adding more milk, if necessary.

3 Turn out the dough onto a lightly floured counter and roll out to a thickness of about ¾ inch/2 cm. Stamp out rounds using a 2¾-inch/7-cm cookie cutter. Press the trimmings together lightly and stamp out more rounds.

4 Place the rounds on the prepared baking sheet and brush the tops lightly with milk. Bake in the preheated oven for 12–15 minutes, until firm and golden brown. Lift onto a wire rack to cool.

5 To make the filling, stir the vanilla extract into the mascarpone cheese with 2 tablespoons of the sugar. Reserve a few whole strawberries for decoration, then hull and slice the remainder. Sprinkle with the remaining sugar.

6 Split the shortcakes in half horizontally. Spoon half of the mascarpone mixture onto the bottom halves and top with sliced strawberries. Spoon over the remaining mascarpone mixture and replace the shortcake tops. To serve, dust with confectioners' sugar and top with the reserved whole strawberries.

IMPRESS THE FAMILY

Oat & Potato Bread

MAKES 1 LOAF

INGREDIENTS

- oil, for greasing
- 2 mealy potatoes
- 3½ cups white bread flour, plus extra for dusting
- 1½ tsp salt
- 3 tbsp butter, diced
- 1½ tsp active dry yeast
- 1½ tbsp dark brown sugar
- 3 tbsp rolled oats
- 2 tbsp skim milk powder
- scant 1 cup lukewarm water

TOPPING

- 1 tbsp water
- 1 tbsp rolled oats

1 Grease a 9 × 5 × 3-inch/ 23 × 13 × 8-cm loaf pan. Put the potatoes in a large saucepan, add water to cover, and bring to a boil. Cook for 20–25 minutes, until tender. Drain, then mash until smooth. Let cool.

2 Sift the flour and salt into a warmed bowl. Rub in the butter with your fingertips. Stir in the yeast, sugar, oats, and milk powder. Mix in the mashed potatoes, then add the water and mix to a soft dough.

3 Turn out the dough onto a lightly floured counter and knead for 5–10 minutes, or until smooth and elastic. Put the dough in an oiled bowl, cover with plastic wrap, and let rise in a warm place for 1 hour, or until doubled in size.

4 Turn out the dough again and knead lightly. Shape into a loaf and transfer to the prepared pan. Cover and let rise in a warm place for 30 minutes. Meanwhile, preheat the oven to 425°F/220°C.

5 For the topping, brush the surface of the loaf with the water and carefully sprinkle over the oats. Bake in the preheated oven for 25–30 minutes, or until the loaf sounds hollow when tapped on the bottom. Transfer to a wire rack and let cool slightly. Serve warm.

GRANDMOTHER'S TIP
Instead of making mashed potatoes from scratch, this is a frugal, yet still delicious, way to use your leftovers.

176

Sourdough Bread

MAKES 2 LOAVES
INGREDIENTS

- 4 cups whole wheat flour
- 4 tsp salt
- 1½ cups lukewarm water
- 2 tbsp molasses
- 1 tbsp vegetable oil, plus extra for brushing
- all-purpose flour, for dusting

STARTER
- ¾ cup whole wheat flour
- ¾ cup white bread flour
- generous ¼ cup superfine sugar
- 1 cup milk

1 First, make the starter. Put the whole wheat flour, white bread flour, sugar, and milk into a nonmetallic bowl and beat well with a fork. Cover with a damp dish towel and let stand at room temperature for 4–5 days, until the mixture is frothy and smells sour.

2 Sift the flour and half of the salt together into a bowl and add the water, molasses, oil, and starter. Mix well with a wooden spoon until a dough begins to form, then knead with your hands until it leaves the side of the bowl. Turn out onto a lightly floured counter and knead for 10 minutes, until smooth and elastic.

3 Brush a bowl with oil. Form the dough into a ball, put it into the bowl, and put the bowl into a plastic bag or cover with a damp dish towel. Let rise in a warm place for 2 hours, until doubled in volume.

4 Dust two cookie sheets with flour. Mix the remaining salt with 4 tablespoons of water in a bowl. Turn out the dough onto a lightly floured counter and punch down with your fist, then knead for an additional 10 minutes. Halve the dough, shape each piece into an oval, and place the loaves on the prepared cookie sheets. Brush with the salt-water glaze and let stand in a warm place, brushing frequently with the glaze, for 30 minutes.

5 Preheat the oven to 425°F/220°C. Brush the loaves with the remaining glaze and bake for 30 minutes, until the crust is golden brown and the loaves sound hollow when tapped on the bottom with your knuckles. If it is necessary to cook them for longer, reduce the oven temperature to 375°F/190°C. Transfer to wire racks to cool.

Cornbread

MAKES 1 SMALL LOAF

INGREDIENTS

- vegetable oil, for brushing
- 1½ cups all-purpose flour
- 1 tsp salt
- 4 tsp baking powder
- 1 tsp superfine sugar
- 2½ cups yellow cornmeal
- ¾ cup butter, softened
- 4 eggs
- 1 cup milk
- 3 tbsp heavy cream

1 Preheat the oven to 400°F/200°C. Brush an 8-inch/20-cm square cake pan with oil.

2 Sift together the flour, salt, and baking powder into a bowl. Add the sugar and cornmeal and stir to mix. Add the butter and cut it into the dry ingredients with a knife, then rub in with your fingertips until the mixture resembles breadcrumbs.

3 Lightly beat the eggs with the milk and cream in a bowl, then stir into the cornmeal mixture until thoroughly combined.

4 Spoon the mixture into the prepared pan and smooth the surface. Bake for 30–35 minutes, until a toothpick inserted into the center of the loaf comes out clean. Remove the pan from the oven and let the bread cool for 5–10 minutes, then cut into squares and serve warm.

PRACTICE MAKES PERFECT

JUST DESSERTS

Banana Cream Pie

SERVES 8–10
INGREDIENTS

- 1¼ cups all-purpose flour, for dusting
- 12 oz/350 g prepared pastry, thawed, if frozen
- 4 extra-large egg yolks
- heaped ¾ cup superfine sugar
- 4 tbsp cornstarch
- pinch of salt
- 2 cups milk
- 1 tsp vanilla extract
- 3 bananas
- ½ tbsp lemon juice
- 1½ cups whipping cream, whipped with 3 tbsp confectioners' sugar, to decorate

1 Preheat the oven to 400°F/200°C. Very lightly flour a rolling pin and use to roll out the dough on a lightly floured counter to a 12-inch/30-cm circle. Line a 9-inch/23-cm pie plate with the dough, then trim the excess dough and prick the bottom all over with a fork. Line the pastry shell with parchment paper and fill with dried beans.

2 Bake in the preheated oven for 15 minutes, or until the pastry is a light golden color. Remove the paper and beans and prick the bottom again. Return to the oven and bake for an additional 5–10 minutes, until golden and dry. Transfer to a wire rack and let cool completely.

3 Meanwhile, put the egg yolks, sugar, cornstarch, and salt into a bowl and beat until blended and pale in color. Beat in the milk and vanilla extract.

4 Pour the mixture into a heavy-bottom saucepan over medium–high heat and bring to a boil, stirring, until smooth and thick. Reduce the heat to low and simmer, stirring, for 2 minutes. Strain the mixture into a bowl and set aside to cool.

5 Slice the bananas, place in a bowl with the lemon juice, and toss. Arrange them in the cooled pastry shell, then top with the custard and let chill in the refrigerator for at least 2 hours. Spread the whipped cream over the top and serve immediately.

GRANDMOTHER'S TIP
Old-fashioned metal pie plates, cake pans, and tart pans conduct heat better than glass, earthenware, or porcelain, producing even baking and reducing the cooking time.

Lemon Meringue Pie

SERVES 6–8

INGREDIENTS

PIE DOUGH

- generous 1 cup all-purpose flour, plus extra for dusting
- 6 tbsp butter, cut into small pieces, plus extra for greasing
- ¼ cup superfine sugar, sifted
- finely grated rind of ½ lemon
- ½ egg yolk, beaten
- 1½ tbsp milk

FILLING

- 3 tbsp cornstarch
- 1¼ cups water
- juice and grated rind of 2 lemons
- generous ¾ cup superfine sugar
- 2 eggs, separated

1 To make the pie dough, sift the flour into a bowl. Rub in the butter, using your fingertips, until the mixture resembles fine breadcrumbs. Mix in the sugar, lemon rind, egg yolk, and milk. Knead briefly on a lightly floured counter. Let rest for 30 minutes.

2 Preheat the oven to 350°F/180°C. Grease an 8-inch/20-cm round tart pan. Roll out the pie dough to a thickness of ¼ inch/5 mm and use it to line the bottom and side of the prepared pan. Prick all over with a fork, line with parchment paper, and fill with dried beans. Bake in the preheated oven for 15 minutes. Remove from the oven and take out the parchment paper and dried beans. Reduce the temperature to 300°F/150°C.

3 To make the filling, mix the cornstarch with a little of the water. Place the remaining water in a saucepan. Stir in the lemon juice and rind and the cornstarch paste. Bring to a boil, stirring. Cook for 2 minutes. Let cool a little. Stir in 5 tablespoons of the sugar and the egg yolks, then pour into the pastry shell.

4 Whip the egg whites in a clean, grease-free bowl until stiff. Whip in the remaining sugar and spread over the pie. Return to the oven and bake for an additional 40 minutes. Remove from the oven, let cool, and serve.

DINNER PARTY WINNER

186

Key Lime Pie

SERVES 8
INGREDIENTS

CRUMB CRUST

- 6 oz/175 g graham crackers or gingersnaps
- 2 tbsp superfine sugar
- ½ tsp ground cinnamon
- 5 tbsp butter, melted, plus extra for greasing

FILLING

- 1¾ cups canned sweetened condensed milk
- ½ cup freshly squeezed lime juice
- finely grated rind of 3 limes
- 4 egg yolks
- whipped cream, to serve

1 Preheat the oven to 325°F/160°C. Lightly grease a 9-inch/23-cm round tart pan, about 1½ inches/4 cm deep.

2 To make the crumb crust, place the crackers, sugar, and cinnamon in a food processor and process until fine crumbs form—do not overprocess to a powder. Add the melted butter and process again until moistened.

3 Tip the crumb mixture into the prepared tart pan and press over the bottom and sides. Place the tart pan on a baking sheet and bake in the preheated oven for 5 minutes.

4 Meanwhile, to make the filling, beat the condensed milk, lime juice, lime rind, and egg yolks together in a bowl until well blended.

5 Remove the tart pan from the oven, pour in the filling, and spread out to the edges. Return to the oven for 15 minutes, or until the filling is set around the edges but still wobbly in the center.

6 Let cool completely on a wire rack, then cover and let chill for at least 2 hours. Serve spread thickly with whipped cream.

Rhubarb Crumble

INGREDIENTS

- 2 lb/900 g rhubarb
- ½ cup superfine sugar
- grated rind and juice of 1 orange
- Homemade Custard (see page 144), to serve

CRUMBLE TOPPING

- scant 1¾ cups all-purpose or whole wheat flour
- ½ cup unsalted butter, diced and chilled
- ½ cup light brown sugar
- 1 tsp ground ginger

1 Preheat the oven to 375°F/190°C.

2 Cut the rhubarb into 1-inch/2.5-cm lengths and put in an ovenproof dish with the sugar and the orange rind and juice.

3 To make the crumble topping, sift the flour into a bowl. Rub in the butter with your fingertips until the mixture resembles fine breadcrumbs. Stir in the sugar and ginger.

4 Spread the crumble topping evenly over the fruit and press down lightly with a fork.

5 Bake in the center of the preheated oven for 25–30 minutes, until the crumble is golden brown. Serve warm with Custard.

GRANDMOTHER'S TIP
Use very young shoots of rhubarb because they are the sweetest. A handful of strawberries would be a good addition, since they enhance the flavor and color.

Bread & Butter Pudding

SERVES 4–6

INGREDIENTS

- 6 tbsp butter, softened
- 6 slices thick white bread
- ⅓ cup mixed dried fruit
- 2 tbsp candied peel
- 3 extra-large eggs
- 1¼ cups milk
- ⅔ cup heavy cream
- ¼ cup superfine sugar
- whole nutmeg, for grating
- 1 tbsp raw sugar
- heavy cream, to serve

1 Preheat the oven to 350°F/180°C.

2 Use a little of the butter to grease an 8 x 10-inch/20 x 25-cm baking dish and butter the slices of bread. Cut the bread into quarters and arrange half overlapping in the dish.

3 Scatter half of the dried fruit and peel over the bread, cover with the remaining bread slices, and add the remaining fruit and peel.

4 In a pitcher, whisk the eggs well and mix in the milk, cream, and sugar. Pour this over the pudding and let stand for 15 minutes to let the bread soak up some of the egg mixture. Tuck in most of the fruit so it doesn't burn in the oven.

5 Grate nutmeg over the top of the pudding to taste, and sprinkle over the raw sugar.

6 Place the dessert on a baking sheet and bake in the top of the oven for 30–40 minutes, until just set and golden brown.

7 Remove from the oven and serve warm with a little cream.

GRANDMOTHER'S TIP
Try using brioche or a lightly fruited loaf instead of white bread. Any mixture of dried fruit can be used, so why not experiment with your favorites?

Baked Rice Pudding

SERVES 4–6

INGREDIENTS

- 1 tbsp melted unsalted butter
- ½ cup white rice
- ¼ cup superfine sugar
- 3½ cups milk
- ½ tsp vanilla extract
- 3 tbsp unsalted butter, chilled and cut into pieces
- whole nutmeg, for grating
- cream, jelly, fresh fruit puree, stewed fruit, honey, or ice cream, to serve

1 Preheat the oven to 300°F/150°C. Grease a 5-cup/1.2-liter baking dish (a gratin dish is good) with the melted butter, place the rice in the dish, and sprinkle with the sugar.

2 Heat the milk in a saucepan until almost boiling, then pour over the rice. Add the vanilla extract and stir well to dissolve the sugar.

3 Scatter the butter over the surface of the pudding.

4 Grate nutmeg to taste over the top, giving it a good covering.

5 Place the dish on a baking sheet and bake in the center of the oven for 1½–2 hours, until the pudding is well browned on top, stirring after the first 30 minutes of cooking to disperse the rice. Serve hot with cream.

GRANDMOTHER'S TIP
When measuring honey or syrup, dip the measuring spoon in hot water and dry it first to prevent sticking.

New York Cheesecake

SERVES 10

INGREDIENTS

- generous ½ cup butter
- 1½ cups finely crushed graham crackers
- 1 tbsp granulated sugar
- 4 cups cream cheese
- 1¼ cups superfine sugar
- 2 tbsp all-purpose flour
- 1 tsp vanilla extract
- finely grated zest of 1 orange
- finely grated zest of 1 lemon
- 3 eggs
- 2 egg yolks
- 1¼ cups heavy cream

1 Preheat the oven to 350°F/180°C. Place a small saucepan over low heat, add the butter, and heat until melted, then remove from the heat, stir in the crackers and granulated sugar, and mix through.

2 Press the cracker mixture tightly into the bottom of a 9-inch/23-cm springform cake pan. Place in the oven and bake for 10 minutes. Remove from the oven and let cool on a wire rack.

3 Increase the oven temperature to 400°F/200°C. With an electric mixer beat the cheese until creamy, then gradually add the superfine sugar and flour and beat until smooth. Increase the speed and beat in the vanilla extract, orange zest, and lemon zest, then beat in the eggs and egg yolks one at a time. Finally, beat in the cream. Scrape any excess into the mixture. It should be light and whippy—beat on a faster setting if you need to.

4 Butter the side of the cake pan and pour in the filling. Smooth the top, transfer to the preheated oven, and bake for 15 minutes, then reduce the temperature to 225°F/110°C and bake for an additional 30 minutes. Turn off the oven and let the cheesecake stand in it for 2 hours to cool and set. Cover and refrigerate overnight.

5 Slide a knife around the edge of the cake, then unfasten the pan, cut the cheesecake into wedge-shape slices, and serve.

GUILTY PLEASURE

Caramel-Topped Date Pudding

SERVES 4

INGREDIENTS

- generous ½ cup golden raisins
- 1 cup chopped pitted dates
- 1 tsp baking soda
- 2 tbsp butter, plus extra for greasing
- 1 cup light brown sugar
- 2 eggs
- 1⅓ cups all-purpose flour, sifted

CARAMEL SAUCE

- 2 tbsp butter
- scant ¾ cup heavy cream
- 1 cup light brown sugar
- zested rind of 1 orange, to decorate
- freshly whipped cream, to serve (optional)

1 Put the golden raisins, dates, and baking soda into a heatproof bowl. Cover with boiling water and let soak.

2 Preheat the oven to 350°F/180°C. Grease a round cake pan, 8 inches/ 20 cm in diameter.

3 Put the butter in a separate bowl, add the sugar and mix well. Beat in the eggs, then fold in the flour. Drain the soaked fruit, add to the bowl, and mix. Spoon the mixture evenly into the prepared cake pan.

4 Transfer to the preheated oven and bake for 35–40 minutes. The pudding is cooked when a skewer inserted into the center comes out clean.

5 About 5 minutes before the end of the cooking time, make the caramel sauce. Melt the butter in a saucepan over medium heat. Stir in the cream and sugar and bring to a boil, stirring continuously. Reduce the heat and let simmer for 5 minutes.

6 Turn out onto a serving plate and pour over the sauce. Decorate with zested orange rind and serve with whipped cream, if using.

GRANDMOTHER'S TIP
You can make this wicked dessert in individual bowls so that everyone has their own portion. Cook for 20–25 minutes and then turn out onto serving plates.

Chocolate Pudding

SERVES 4–6

INGREDIENTS

- ½ cup sugar
- 4 tbsp unsweetened cocoa
- 2 tbsp cornstarch
- pinch of salt
- 1½ cups milk
- 1 extra-large egg, beaten
- 4 tbsp butter
- ½ tsp vanilla extract
- heavy cream,
  to serve (optional)

1 Put the sugar, cocoa, cornstarch, and salt into a heatproof bowl, stir, and set aside.

2 Pour the milk into a saucepan and heat over medium heat until just simmering. Do not bring to a boil.

3 Keeping the pan over medium heat, spoon a little of the simmering milk into the sugar mixture and blend, then stir this mixture into the milk in the pan. Beat in the egg and half of the butter and reduce the heat to low.

4 Simmer for 5–8 minutes, stirring frequently, until the mixture thickens. Remove from the heat and add the vanilla extract and the remaining butter, stirring until the butter melts and is absorbed.

5 The pudding can be served either hot or chilled, with cream for pouring over. If chilling the pudding, spoon it into a serving bowl and let cool completely, then press plastic wrap onto the surface to prevent a skin from forming and chill in the refrigerator until required.

Fudge

MAKES 32 PIECES

INGREDIENTS

- 2 tbsp unsweetened cocoa
- 1¼ cups milk
- 4½ oz/125 g bittersweet
  chocolate, at least
  85 percent cocoa solids,
  finely chopped
- 4 cups superfine sugar
- ½ cup butter, chopped,
  plus extra for greasing
- pinch of salt
- 1½ tsp vanilla extract
- 1¾ cups pecans, walnuts,
  or toasted hazelnuts, or a
  mixture of nuts, chopped

1 Put the cocoa into a small bowl, add 2 tablespoons of the milk, and stir until blended. Pour the remaining milk into a large, heavy-bottom saucepan, then add the cocoa mixture and chocolate and simmer over medium–high heat, stirring, until the chocolate melts. Add the sugar, butter, and salt, reduce the heat to low, and stir until the butter is melted, the sugar is dissolved, and you can't feel any of the grains when you rub a spoon against the side of the pan.

2 Increase the heat and bring the milk to a boil. Cover the pan and boil for 2 minutes, then uncover and carefully clip a candy thermometer to the side. Continue boiling, without stirring, until the temperature reaches 247°F/115°C, or until a small amount of the mixture forms a soft ball when dropped in cold water.

3 Meanwhile, line an 8-inch/20-cm square cake pan with foil, grease the foil, and set aside.

4 Remove the saucepan from the heat, stir in the vanilla extract, and beat the fudge until it thickens. Stir in the nuts.

5 Pour the fudge mixture into the prepared pan and use a wet spatula to smooth the surface. Set aside and let stand for at least 2 hours to become firm. Lift the fudge out of the pan, then peel off the foil. Cut the fudge into eight 1-inch/2.5-cm strips, then cut each strip into four pieces. Store the fudge for up to 1 week in an airtight container.

Pecan Pie

SERVES 8

INGREDIENTS

PIE DOUGH
- 1¾ cups all-purpose flour, plus extra for dusting
- ½ cup butter
- 2 tbsp superfine sugar
- a little cold water

FILLING
- 5 tbsp butter
- scant ½ cup light brown sugar
- ⅔ cup light corn syrup
- 2 extra-large eggs, beaten
- 1 tsp vanilla extract
- 1 cup pecans

1 To make the pie dough, place the flour in a bowl and rub in the butter using your fingertips until it resembles fine breadcrumbs. Stir in the sugar and add enough cold water to mix to a firm dough. Wrap in plastic wrap and chill for 15 minutes, until firm enough to roll out.

2 Preheat the oven to 400°F/200°C. Roll out the dough on a lightly floured counter and use to line a 9-inch/23-cm loose-bottom round tart pan. Prick the bottom with a fork. Chill for 15 minutes.

3 Place the tart pan on a baking sheet and line with a sheet of parchment paper and dried beans. Bake in the preheated oven for 10 minutes. Remove the paper and beans and bake for an additional 5 minutes. Reduce the oven temperature to 350°F/180°C.

4 To make the filling, place the butter, sugar, and corn syrup in a saucepan and heat gently until melted. Remove from the heat and quickly beat in the eggs and vanilla extract.

5 Coarsely chop the pecans and stir into the mixture. Pour into the tart shell and bake for 35–40 minutes, until the filling is just set. Serve warm or cold.

GRANDMOTHER'S TIP
Add 2 tablespoons of dark rum to the filling just before removing it from the heat. This will balance the sweetness and bring out the rich flavors.

Pumpkin Pie

SERVES 6
INGREDIENTS

- 4 lb/1.8 kg sweet pumpkin
- 1 cup all-purpose flour, plus extra for dusting
- ¼ tsp baking powder
- 1½ tsp ground cinnamon
- ¾ tsp ground nutmeg
- ¾ tsp ground cloves
- 1 tsp salt
- ½ cup superfine sugar
- 4 tbsp cold unsalted butter, diced, plus extra for greasing
- 3 eggs
- 1¾ cups canned sweetened condensed milk
- ½ tsp vanilla extract
- 1 tbsp raw brown sugar

STREUSEL TOPPING
- 2 tbsp all-purpose flour
- 4 tbsp raw brown sugar
- 1 tsp ground cinnamon
- 2 tbsp cold unsalted butter, cut into small pieces
- generous ⅔ cup chopped pecans
- generous ⅔ cup chopped walnuts

1 Preheat the oven to 375°F/190°C. Halve the pumpkin, then remove and discard the stem, seeds, and stringy insides. Put the pumpkin halves, face down, in a shallow roasting pan and cover with foil. Bake in the preheated oven for 1½ hours, then let cool. Scoop out the flesh and puree in a food processor. Drain off any excess liquid. Cover with plastic wrap and chill until ready to use.

2 Grease a 9-inch/23-cm round pie pan. Sift the flour and baking powder into a large bowl. Stir in ½ teaspoon of the cinnamon, ¼ teaspoon of the nutmeg, ¼ teaspoon of the cloves, ½ teaspoon of the salt, and all of the superfine sugar.

3 Rub in the butter with your fingertips until the mixture resembles fine breadcrumbs, then make a well in the center. Lightly beat 1 of the eggs and pour it into the well. Mix together with a wooden spoon, then use your hands to shape the dough into a ball. Place the dough on a lightly floured counter and roll out to a round large enough to line the pie pan. Use it to line the pan, then trim the edges. Cover with plastic wrap and chill in the refrigerator for 30 minutes.

4 Preheat the oven to 425°F/220°C. To make the filling, put the pumpkin puree in a large bowl, then stir in the condensed milk and the remaining eggs. Add the remaining spices and salt, then stir in the vanilla extract and brown sugar. Pour into the pastry shell and bake in the preheated oven for 15 minutes.

5 Meanwhile, make the streusel topping. Combine the flour, sugar, and cinnamon in a bowl, rub in the butter, then stir in the nuts. Remove the pie from the oven and reduce the heat to 350°F/180°C. Sprinkle over the topping, then bake for an additional 35 minutes.

IMPRESS THE FAMILY

Sweet Potato Pie

INGREDIENTS

PIE DOUGH

- 1¼ cups all-purpose flour, plus extra for dusting
- ½ tsp salt
- ¼ tsp superfine sugar
- 1½ tbsp butter, diced
- 3 tbsp shortening, diced
- 2–2½ tbsp cold water

FILLING

- 1 lb 2 oz/500 g orange-flesh sweet potatoes, peeled
- 3 extra-large eggs, beaten
- ½ cup firmly packed light brown sugar
- 1½ cups canned condensed milk
- 3 tbsp butter, melted
- 2 tsp vanilla extract
- 1 tsp ground cinnamon
- 1 tsp ground nutmeg
- ½ tsp salt

1 To make the pie dough, sift the flour, salt, and sugar into a bowl. Add the butter and shortening to the bowl and rub in with your fingertips until the mixture resembles fine breadcrumbs. Sprinkle over 2 tablespoons of the water and mix with a fork to make a soft dough. If the dough is too dry, sprinkle in the extra ½ tablespoon of water. Wrap the dough in plastic wrap and chill in the refrigerator for at least 1 hour.

2 Meanwhile, bring a large saucepan of water to a boil over high heat. Add the sweet potatoes and cook for 15 minutes. Drain, then cool under cold running water. When cool, cut each potato into eight wedges. Place the potatoes in a bowl and beat in the eggs and sugar until very smooth. Beat in the remaining ingredients, then set aside until required.

3 Preheat the oven to 425°F/220°C. Roll out the pie dough on a lightly floured counter into a thin 11-inch/28-cm round and use to line a 9-inch/23-cm round tart pan, about 1½ inches/4 cm deep. Trim off the excess dough and press a floured fork around the edge.

4 Prick the bottom of the pastry shell all over with the fork. Line with parchment paper and fill with dried beans. Bake in the preheated oven for 12 minutes, until lightly golden. Remove from the oven and take out the paper and beans.

5 Pour the filling into the pastry shell and return to the oven for an additional 10 minutes. Reduce the oven temperature to 325°F/160°C and bake for an additional 35 minutes, or until a knife inserted into the center comes out clean. Let cool on a wire rack. Serve warm or at room temperature.

Indian Pudding

INGREDIENTS

- 2 tbsp raisins or golden raisins
- 5 tbsp coarse yellow cornmeal
- 1½ cups milk
- 4 tbsp dark molasses
- 2 tbsp dark brown sugar
- ½ tbsp salt
- 2 tbsp butter, diced, plus extra for greasing
- 2 tsp ground ginger
- ¼ tsp cinnamon
- ¼ tsp ground nutmeg
- 2 eggs, beaten
- vanilla ice cream or maple syrup, to serve

1 Preheat the oven to 300°F/150°C. Generously butter a 4-cup/900-ml baking dish that is suitable for serving from and set aside. Put the raisins in a strainer with 1 tablespoon of the cornmeal and toss well together. Shake off the excess cornmeal and set aside.

2 Put the milk and molasses into a saucepan over medium–high heat and stir until the molasses is dissolved. Add the sugar and salt and continue stirring until the sugar is dissolved. Sprinkle the remaining cornmeal over and bring to a boil, stirring continuously. Reduce the heat and simmer for 3–5 minutes, until the mixture is thickened.

3 Remove the pan from the heat, add the butter, ginger, cinnamon, and nutmeg and stir until the butter is melted. Add the eggs and beat until they are incorporated, then stir in the raisins. Pour the batter into the prepared dish.

4 Put the dish in a small roasting pan and pour in enough boiling water to come halfway up the side of the dish. Put the dish in the preheated oven and bake, uncovered, for 1¾–2 hours, until the pudding is set and a toothpick inserted in the center comes out clean.

5 Serve immediately, straight from the dish, with a dollop of ice cream on top.

Apple Turnovers

INGREDIENTS

- 9 oz/250 g prepared
  puff pastry, thawed, if frozen
- milk, for glazing

FILLING

- 1 lb/450 g baking apples,
  peeled, cored, and chopped
- grated rind of
  1 lemon (optional)
- pinch of ground
  cloves (optional)
- 3 tbsp sugar

ORANGE SUGAR

- 1 tbsp sugar, for sprinkling
- finely grated rind of
  1 orange

ORANGE CREAM

- 1 cup heavy cream
- grated rind of 1 orange and
  juice of ½ orange
- confectioners' sugar, to taste

1 Prepare the filling before rolling out the pastry. Mix together the apples, lemon rind, and cloves, if using, but do not add the sugar until the last minute because this will cause the juice to seep out of the apples. To make the orange sugar, mix the sugar and orange rind together.

2 Preheat the oven to 425°F/220°C. Roll out the pastry on a floured counter into a rectangle measuring 24 × 12 inches/ 60 × 30 cm. Cut the pastry in half lengthwise, then across into four to make eight 6-inch/15-cm squares. (You can do this in two batches, rolling out half of the pastry into a 12-inch/30-cm square and cutting it into quarters, if preferred.)

3 Mix the sugar into the apple filling. Brush each square lightly with milk and place a little of the apple filling in the center. Fold over one corner diagonally to meet the opposite one, making a triangular turnover, and press the edges together very firmly. Place on a nonstick baking sheet. Repeat with the remaining squares.

4 Brush the turnovers with milk and sprinkle with a little of the orange sugar. Bake for 15–20 minutes, until puffed and well browned. Cool the turnovers on a wire rack.

5 To make the orange cream, whip the cream and the orange rind and juice together until thick. Add a little sugar to taste and whip again until the cream just holds soft peaks. Serve the warm turnovers with dollops of orange cream.

GRANDMOTHER'S TIP
For something extra warming, try adding some cinnamon, or replace the lemon rind with orange rind and a teaspoon of marmalade.

Apple Fritters

MAKES 12 FRITTERS

INGREDIENTS

- 2¾ cups peeled, cored, and diced apples, such as Granny Smith
- 1 tsp lemon juice
- 2 eggs, separated
- ⅔ cup milk
- 1 tbsp butter, melted
- ½ cup all-purpose flour
- ½ cup whole wheat flour
- 2 tbsp sugar
- ¼ tsp salt
- sunflower oil, for deep-frying and greasing

CINNAMON GLAZE

- ½ cup confectioners' sugar
- ½ tsp cinnamon
- 1 tbsp milk, plus extra, if needed

1 To make the cinnamon glaze, sift the sugar and cinnamon into a small bowl and make a well in the center. Slowly stir in the milk until smooth, then set aside.

2 Put the apples in a small bowl, add the lemon juice, toss, and set aside. Beat the egg whites in a separate bowl until stiff peaks form and set aside.

3 Heat enough oil for deep-frying in a deep-fat fryer or heavy-bottom saucepan until it reaches 350°F/180°C, or until a cube of bread browns in 30 seconds.

4 Meanwhile, put the egg yolks and milk into a large bowl and beat together, then stir in the butter. Sift in the all-purpose flour, whole wheat flour, sugar, and salt, adding in any bran left in the sifter, then stir the dry ingredients into the

wet ingredients until just combined. Stir in the apples and their juices, then fold in the egg whites.

5 Use a greased spoon to drop spoonfuls of batter into the hot oil, without overcrowding the fryer, and fry for 2–3 minutes, turning once, until the fritters are golden brown on both sides. Transfer the fritters to paper towels to drain, then transfer to a wire rack. Repeat this process until all the batter is used.

6 Stir the glaze and add a little extra milk, if necessary, so it flows freely from the tip of a spoon. Drizzle the glaze over the fritters and let stand for 3–5 minutes to firm up. Serve immediately.

GRANDMOTHER'S TIP
If not serving the fritters immediately, sift over some confectioners' sugar, cinnamon, and a pinch of nutmeg, then let cool. However, these are best eaten on the day they are made.

Banana Splits

SERVES 4

INGREDIENTS

- 4 bananas
- 6 tbsp chopped mixed nuts, to serve

VANILLA ICE CREAM

- 1¼ cups milk
- 1 tsp vanilla extract
- 3 egg yolks
- ½ cup superfine sugar
- 1¼ cups heavy cream, whipped

CHOCOLATE RUM SAUCE

- 4½ oz/125 g semisweet chocolate, broken into small pieces
- 2½ tbsp butter
- 6 tbsp water
- 1 tbsp rum

1 To make the vanilla ice cream, heat the milk and vanilla extract in a saucepan until almost boiling. Put the egg yolks and sugar into a bowl and beat together. Remove the milk from the heat and stir a little into the egg mixture. Transfer the mixture to the pan. Stir over low heat until thick. Do not boil. Remove from the heat.

2 Let cool for 30 minutes, fold in the cream, cover with plastic wrap, and chill for 1 hour. Transfer to an ice-cream maker and process for 15 minutes.

3 Alternatively, transfer into a freezerproof container and freeze for 1 hour, then place in a bowl and beat to break up the ice crystals. Put back in the container and freeze for 30 minutes. Repeat twice more, freezing for 30 minutes and beating each time.

4 To make the chocolate rum sauce, melt the chocolate and butter with the water in a saucepan, stirring continuously. Remove from the heat and stir in the rum. Peel the bananas, slice them lengthwise, and arrange in 4 serving dishes. Top with ice cream and nuts and serve with the sauce.

GRANDMOTHER'S TIP
For a quick and easy dessert, use store-bought ice cream. If you're serving the banana splits to children, omit the rum from the chocolate sauce.

Created with
love by
....

Baked with love
by
....

TRY THESE TASTY
....
DATE MADE
....
INGREDIENTS
....
....

Baked with
love by
....

Created with love by
....

TRY THESE TASTY
....
DATE MADE
....
INGREDIENTS
....
....
....

Baked with
love by
....

Created with love
by
....

Baked with love
by
....

TRY THESE TASTY
....
DATE MADE
....
INGREDIENTS
....
....

Baked with
love by
....

Created with love by
....

Created with love by
....

Baked with
love by
....

Created with love
by
....

Baked with love by
....

Created with
love by
....

Baked with
love by
....

Baked with
love by
....

TRY THESE TASTY
....
DATE MADE
....
INGREDIENTS
....
....
....
....

Created with love by
....

TRY THESE TASTY
....
DATE MADE
....
INGREDIENTS
....
....
....
....

Baked with love
by
....

TRY THESE TASTY
....
DATE MADE
....
INGREDIENTS
....
....

fond memories xx